THIS BOOK BELONGS TO:

CONTACT INFORMATION	
NAME:	
ADDRESS:	
PHONE:	

START / END DATES

___ / ___ / ___ TO ___ / ___ / ___

Dedication

This Barrel Racing Log Journal is dedicated to all the rodeo enthusiasts out there who want to record their barrel racing events and document their findings in the process.

You are my inspiration for producing books and I'm honored to be a part of keeping all of your barrel racing notes and records organized.

This journal notebook will help you record the details of your rodeo adventures.

Thoughtfully put together with these sections to record: Event Information, Health Requirements, Conditions, Horse Name, Pre-Run, Notes, Need To Work On, Equipment, Results, and Likes & Dislikes.

How to Use this Book

The purpose of this book is to keep all of your Barrel Racing notes all in one place. It will help keep you organized.

This Barrel Racing Log Journal will allow you to accurately document every detail about your barrel racing adventures.

Here are examples of the prompts for you to fill in and write about your experience in this book:

1. Event Information - Write Name of Race Event, Date, Time, Miles Away, Location, Entry Fee, Side Pot, Time Outs Allowed, Stalls Available, Call In Date, Confirmation Number, Buddy, Draw.

2. Health Requirements Log any health requirements for your horse.

3. Conditions - For writing Gate, Ground Type, Position On The Ground, Weather Conditions, Temperature, Indoor or Outdoor, Run In, Set Up, Slack/ Performance, Daylight or Lighted, Other Pen Notes.

4. Horse Name - Log the name of the horse.

5. Pre-Run - Record your pre-run time, any side pot info, and pre-run routine.

6. Run Notes - Write any important information about your run.

7. Need To Work On - Log anything you need to work on for next time.

8. Equipment - Record any equipment you used or was available to use.

9. Winning Results - Write the times and payout for winners and the number of entries.

10. Likes & Dislikes About The Event - Record what you like and didn't like about the event.

Rodeo Racing / Jackpot

NAME	

SANCTION / ASSOCIATION		DATE		TIME	:
LOCATION		MILES AWAY			
ENTRY FEE	$	ADDED MONEY	$		
SIDE POT Y/N TYPE		ENTRY FEE	$	ADDED MONEY	$
SIDE POT Y/N TYPE		ENTRY FEE	$	ADDED MONEY	$
TIME OUTS ALLOWED	○ YES ○ NO	STALLS AVAILABLE	○ YES ○ NO	FEE	$
ENTER: ON SITE / CALL IN DATE		TIME	:	PHONE	
BUDDY		CONFIRMATION #		CALL BACK	
DRAW					

HEALTH REQUIREMENTS

GATE		RUN IN / SET UP	
GROUND TYPE			
GROUND CONDITION			
POSITION ON THE GROUND			
WEATHER CONDITIONS			
TEMPERATURE		SLACK / PERFORMANCE	
INDOOR / OUTDOOR		DAYLIGHT / LIGHTED	
OTHER PEN NOTES			

RESULTS

WINNING TIME	ID		PAYOUT	
	2D		PAYOUT	
	3D		PAYOUT	
	4D		PAYOUT	
	5D		PAYOUT	
			PAYOUT	
			PAYOUT	
PLACES PAID OUT			NUMBER OF ENTRIES	

Rodeo Racing / Jackpot

NAME	

SANCTION / ASSOCIATION		DATE		TIME	:
LOCATION		MILES AWAY			
ENTRY FEE	$	ADDED MONEY	$		
SIDE POT Y/N TYPE		ENTRY FEE	$	ADDED MONEY	$
SIDE POT Y/N TYPE		ENTRY FEE	$	ADDED MONEY	$
TIME OUTS ALLOWED	○ YES ○ NO	STALLS AVAILABLE	○ YES ○ NO	FEE	$
ENTER: ON SITE / CALL IN DATE		TIME	:	PHONE	
BUDDY		CONFIRMATION #		CALL BACK	
DRAW					

HEALTH REQUIREMENTS

GATE		RUN IN / SET UP	
GROUND TYPE			
GROUND CONDITION			
POSITION ON THE GROUND			
WEATHER CONDITIONS			
TEMPERATURE		SLACK / PERFORMANCE	
INDOOR / OUTDOOR		DAYLIGHT / LIGHTED	
OTHER PEN NOTES			

RESULTS

WINNING TIME	ID		PAYOUT	
	2D		PAYOUT	
	3D		PAYOUT	
	4D		PAYOUT	
	5D		PAYOUT	
			PAYOUT	
			PAYOUT	
PLACES PAID OUT			NUMBER OF ENTRIES	

Rodeo Racing / Jackpot

NAME	

SANCTION / ASSOCIATION		DATE		TIME	:
LOCATION		MILES AWAY			
ENTRY FEE	$	ADDED MONEY	$		
SIDE POT Y/N TYPE		ENTRY FEE	$	ADDED MONEY	$
SIDE POT Y/N TYPE		ENTRY FEE	$	ADDED MONEY	$
TIME OUTS ALLOWED	○ YES ○ NO	STALLS AVAILABLE	○ YES ○ NO	FEE	$
ENTER: ON SITE / CALL IN DATE		TIME	:	PHONE	
BUDDY		CONFIRMATION #		CALL BACK	
DRAW					

HEALTH REQUIREMENTS

GATE		RUN IN / SET UP	
GROUND TYPE			
GROUND CONDITION			
POSITION ON THE GROUND			
WEATHER CONDITIONS			
TEMPERATURE		SLACK / PERFORMANCE	
INDOOR / OUTDOOR		DAYLIGHT / LIGHTED	
OTHER PEN NOTES			

RESULTS

WINNING TIME	ID		PAYOUT	
	2D		PAYOUT	
	3D		PAYOUT	
	4D		PAYOUT	
	5D		PAYOUT	
			PAYOUT	
			PAYOUT	
PLACES PAID OUT			NUMBER OF ENTRIES	

Rodeo Racing / Jackpot

NAME	

SANCTION / ASSOCIATION		DATE		TIME	:
LOCATION		MILES AWAY			
ENTRY FEE	$	ADDED MONEY	$		
SIDE POT Y/N TYPE		ENTRY FEE	$	ADDED MONEY	$
SIDE POT Y/N TYPE		ENTRY FEE	$	ADDED MONEY	$
TIME OUTS ALLOWED	○ YES ○ NO	STALLS AVAILABLE	○ YES ○ NO	FEE	$
ENTER: ON SITE / CALL IN DATE		TIME	:	PHONE	
BUDDY		CONFIRMATION #		CALL BACK	
DRAW					

HEALTH REQUIREMENTS

GATE		RUN IN / SET UP	
GROUND TYPE			
GROUND CONDITION			
POSITION ON THE GROUND			
WEATHER CONDITIONS			
TEMPERATURE		SLACK / PERFORMANCE	
INDOOR / OUTDOOR		DAYLIGHT / LIGHTED	
OTHER PEN NOTES			

RESULTS

WINNING TIME			PAYOUT	
	1D		PAYOUT	
	2D		PAYOUT	
	3D		PAYOUT	
	4D		PAYOUT	
	5D		PAYOUT	
			PAYOUT	
			PAYOUT	
PLACES PAID OUT			NUMBER OF ENTRIES	

Rodeo Racing / Jackpot

NAME	

SANCTION / ASSOCIATION		DATE		TIME	:
LOCATION		MILES AWAY			
ENTRY FEE	$	ADDED MONEY	$		
SIDE POT Y/N TYPE		ENTRY FEE	$	ADDED MONEY	$
SIDE POT Y/N TYPE		ENTRY FEE	$	ADDED MONEY	$
TIME OUTS ALLOWED	○ YES ○ NO	STALLS AVAILABLE	○ YES ○ NO	FEE	$
ENTER: ON SITE / CALL IN DATE		TIME	:	PHONE	
BUDDY		CONFIRMATION #		CALL BACK	
DRAW					

HEALTH REQUIREMENTS

GATE		RUN IN / SET UP	
GROUND TYPE			
GROUND CONDITION			
POSITION ON THE GROUND			
WEATHER CONDITIONS			
TEMPERATURE		SLACK / PERFORMANCE	
INDOOR / OUTDOOR		DAYLIGHT / LIGHTED	
OTHER PEN NOTES			

RESULTS

WINNING TIME	ID		PAYOUT	
	2D		PAYOUT	
	3D		PAYOUT	
	4D		PAYOUT	
	5D		PAYOUT	
			PAYOUT	
			PAYOUT	
PLACES PAID OUT			NUMBER OF ENTRIES	

Rodeo Racing / Jackpot

NAME	

SANCTION / ASSOCIATION		DATE		TIME		:
LOCATION		MILES AWAY				
ENTRY FEE	$	ADDED MONEY	$			
SIDE POT Y/N TYPE		ENTRY FEE	$	ADDED MONEY	$	
SIDE POT Y/N TYPE		ENTRY FEE	$	ADDED MONEY	$	
TIME OUTS ALLOWED	○ YES ○ NO	STALLS AVAILABLE	○ YES ○ NO	FEE	$	
ENTER: ON SITE / CALL IN DATE		TIME	:	PHONE		
BUDDY		CONFIRMATION #		CALL BACK		
DRAW						

HEALTH REQUIREMENTS

GATE	RUN IN / SET UP	
GROUND TYPE		
GROUND CONDITION		
POSITION ON THE GROUND		
WEATHER CONDITIONS		
TEMPERATURE	SLACK / PERFORMANCE	
INDOOR / OUTDOOR	DAYLIGHT / LIGHTED	
OTHER PEN NOTES		

RESULTS				
WINNING TIME	1D		PAYOUT	
	2D		PAYOUT	
	3D		PAYOUT	
	4D		PAYOUT	
	5D		PAYOUT	
			PAYOUT	
			PAYOUT	
PLACES PAID OUT			NUMBER OF ENTRIES	

Rodeo Racing / Jackpot

NAME	

SANCTION / ASSOCIATION		DATE		TIME	:
LOCATION		MILES AWAY			
ENTRY FEE	$	ADDED MONEY	$		
SIDE POT Y/N TYPE		ENTRY FEE	$	ADDED MONEY	$
SIDE POT Y/N TYPE		ENTRY FEE	$	ADDED MONEY	$
TIME OUTS ALLOWED	○ YES ○ NO	STALLS AVAILABLE	○ YES ○ NO	FEE	$
ENTER: ON SITE / CALL IN DATE		TIME	:	PHONE	
BUDDY		CONFIRMATION #		CALL BACK	
DRAW					

HEALTH REQUIREMENTS

GATE		RUN IN / SET UP	
GROUND TYPE			
GROUND CONDITION			
POSITION ON THE GROUND			
WEATHER CONDITIONS			
TEMPERATURE		SLACK / PERFORMANCE	
INDOOR / OUTDOOR		DAYLIGHT / LIGHTED	
OTHER PEN NOTES			

RESULTS

WINNING TIME	ID		PAYOUT	
	2D		PAYOUT	
	3D		PAYOUT	
	4D		PAYOUT	
	5D		PAYOUT	
			PAYOUT	
			PAYOUT	
PLACES PAID OUT			NUMBER OF ENTRIES	

Rodeo Racing / Jackpot

NAME	
SANCTION / ASSOCIATION	DATE	TIME :
LOCATION	MILES AWAY	
ENTRY FEE $	ADDED MONEY $	
SIDE POT Y/N TYPE	ENTRY FEE $	ADDED MONEY $
SIDE POT Y/N TYPE	ENTRY FEE $	ADDED MONEY $
TIME OUTS ALLOWED o YES o NO	STALLS AVAILABLE o YES o NO	FEE $
ENTER: ON SITE / CALL IN DATE	TIME :	PHONE
BUDDY	CONFIRMATION #	CALL BACK
DRAW		

HEALTH REQUIREMENTS

GATE	RUN IN / SET UP
GROUND TYPE	
GROUND CONDITION	
POSITION ON THE GROUND	
WEATHER CONDITIONS	
TEMPERATURE	SLACK / PERFORMANCE
INDOOR / OUTDOOR	DAYLIGHT / LIGHTED
OTHER PEN NOTES	

RESULTS

WINNING TIME	1D		PAYOUT	
	2D		PAYOUT	
	3D		PAYOUT	
	4D		PAYOUT	
	5D		PAYOUT	
			PAYOUT	
			PAYOUT	
PLACES PAID OUT			NUMBER OF ENTRIES	

Rodeo Racing / Jackpot

NAME	

SANCTION / ASSOCIATION		DATE		TIME	:
LOCATION		MILES AWAY			
ENTRY FEE	$	ADDED MONEY	$		
SIDE POT Y/N TYPE		ENTRY FEE	$	ADDED MONEY	$
SIDE POT Y/N TYPE		ENTRY FEE	$	ADDED MONEY	$
TIME OUTS ALLOWED	○ YES ○ NO	STALLS AVAILABLE	○ YES ○ NO	FEE	$
ENTER: ON SITE / CALL IN DATE		TIME	:	PHONE	
BUDDY		CONFIRMATION #		CALL BACK	
DRAW					

HEALTH REQUIREMENTS

GATE		RUN IN / SET UP	
GROUND TYPE			
GROUND CONDITION			
POSITION ON THE GROUND			
WEATHER CONDITIONS			
TEMPERATURE		SLACK / PERFORMANCE	
INDOOR / OUTDOOR		DAYLIGHT / LIGHTED	
OTHER PEN NOTES			

RESULTS

WINNING TIME	ID			
	2D		PAYOUT	
	3D		PAYOUT	
	4D		PAYOUT	
	5D		PAYOUT	
			PAYOUT	
			PAYOUT	
			PAYOUT	
PLACES PAID OUT			NUMBER OF ENTRIES	

Rodeo Racing / Jackpot

NAME					
SANCTION / ASSOCIATION		DATE		TIME	:
LOCATION		MILES AWAY			
ENTRY FEE	$	ADDED MONEY	$		
SIDE POT Y/N TYPE		ENTRY FEE	$	ADDED MONEY	$
SIDE POT Y/N TYPE		ENTRY FEE	$	ADDED MONEY	$
TIME OUTS ALLOWED	○ YES ○ NO	STALLS AVAILABLE	○ YES ○ NO	FEE	$
ENTER: ON SITE / CALL IN DATE		TIME	:	PHONE	
BUDDY		CONFIRMATION #		CALL BACK	
DRAW					

HEALTH REQUIREMENTS

GATE		RUN IN / SET UP	
GROUND TYPE			
GROUND CONDITION			
POSITION ON THE GROUND			
WEATHER CONDITIONS			
TEMPERATURE		SLACK / PERFORMANCE	
INDOOR / OUTDOOR		DAYLIGHT / LIGHTED	
OTHER PEN NOTES			

RESULTS

WINNING TIME	ID		PAYOUT	
	1D		PAYOUT	
	2D		PAYOUT	
	3D		PAYOUT	
	4D		PAYOUT	
	5D		PAYOUT	
			PAYOUT	
			PAYOUT	
PLACES PAID OUT			NUMBER OF ENTRIES	

Rodeo Racing / Jackpot

NAME	

SANCTION / ASSOCIATION		DATE		TIME	
LOCATION		MILES AWAY			
ENTRY FEE	$	ADDED MONEY	$		
SIDE POT Y/N TYPE		ENTRY FEE	$	ADDED MONEY	$
SIDE POT Y/N TYPE		ENTRY FEE	$	ADDED MONEY	$
TIME OUTS ALLOWED	○ YES ○ NO	STALLS AVAILABLE	○ YES ○ NO	FEE	$
ENTER: ON SITE / CALL IN DATE		TIME	:	PHONE	
BUDDY		CONFIRMATION #		CALL BACK	
DRAW					

HEALTH REQUIREMENTS

GATE		RUN IN / SET UP	
GROUND TYPE			
GROUND CONDITION			
POSITION ON THE GROUND			
WEATHER CONDITIONS			
TEMPERATURE		SLACK / PERFORMANCE	
INDOOR / OUTDOOR		DAYLIGHT / LIGHTED	
OTHER PEN NOTES			

RESULTS

WINNING TIME	ID		PAYOUT	
	2D		PAYOUT	
	3D		PAYOUT	
	4D		PAYOUT	
	5D		PAYOUT	
			PAYOUT	
			PAYOUT	
PLACES PAID OUT			NUMBER OF ENTRIES	

Rodeo Racing / Jackpot

NAME	

SANCTION / ASSOCIATION		DATE		TIME	
LOCATION		MILES AWAY			
ENTRY FEE	$	ADDED MONEY	$		
SIDE POT Y/N TYPE		ENTRY FEE	$	ADDED MONEY	$
SIDE POT Y/N TYPE		ENTRY FEE	$	ADDED MONEY	$
TIME OUTS ALLOWED	○ YES ○ NO	STALLS AVAILABLE	○ YES ○ NO	FEE	$
ENTER: ON SITE / CALL IN DATE		TIME	:	PHONE	
BUDDY		CONFIRMATION #		CALL BACK	
DRAW					

HEALTH REQUIREMENTS	

GATE		RUN IN / SET UP	
GROUND TYPE			
GROUND CONDITION			
POSITION ON THE GROUND			
WEATHER CONDITIONS			
TEMPERATURE		SLACK / PERFORMANCE	
INDOOR / OUTDOOR		DAYLIGHT / LIGHTED	
OTHER PEN NOTES			

RESULTS

WINNING TIME	1D		PAYOUT	
	2D		PAYOUT	
	3D		PAYOUT	
	4D		PAYOUT	
	5D		PAYOUT	
			PAYOUT	
			PAYOUT	
PLACES PAID OUT			NUMBER OF ENTRIES	

Rodeo Racing / Jackpot

NAME	

SANCTION / ASSOCIATION		DATE		TIME	:
LOCATION		MILES AWAY			
ENTRY FEE	$	ADDED MONEY	$		
SIDE POT Y/N TYPE		ENTRY FEE	$	ADDED MONEY	$
SIDE POT Y/N TYPE		ENTRY FEE	$	ADDED MONEY	$
TIME OUTS ALLOWED	○ YES ○ NO	STALLS AVAILABLE	○ YES ○ NO	FEE	$
ENTER: ON SITE / CALL IN DATE		TIME	:	PHONE	
BUDDY		CONFIRMATION #		CALL BACK	
DRAW					

HEALTH REQUIREMENTS	

GATE		RUN IN / SET UP	
GROUND TYPE			
GROUND CONDITION			
POSITION ON THE GROUND			
WEATHER CONDITIONS			
TEMPERATURE		SLACK / PERFORMANCE	
INDOOR / OUTDOOR		DAYLIGHT / LIGHTED	
OTHER PEN NOTES			

RESULTS

WINNING TIME	ID		PAYOUT	
	2D		PAYOUT	
	3D		PAYOUT	
	4D		PAYOUT	
	5D		PAYOUT	
			PAYOUT	
			PAYOUT	
PLACES PAID OUT			NUMBER OF ENTRIES	

Rodeo Racing / Jackpot

NAME	

SANCTION / ASSOCIATION		DATE		TIME	:
LOCATION		MILES AWAY			
ENTRY FEE	$	ADDED MONEY	$		
SIDE POT Y/N TYPE		ENTRY FEE	$	ADDED MONEY	$
SIDE POT Y/N TYPE		ENTRY FEE	$	ADDED MONEY	$
TIME OUTS ALLOWED	○ YES ○ NO	STALLS AVAILABLE	○ YES ○ NO	FEE	$
ENTER: ON SITE / CALL IN DATE		TIME	:	PHONE	
BUDDY		CONFIRMATION #		CALL BACK	
DRAW					

HEALTH REQUIREMENTS

GATE	
GROUND TYPE	
GROUND CONDITION	
POSITION ON THE GROUND	
WEATHER CONDITIONS	
TEMPERATURE	
INDOOR / OUTDOOR	
OTHER PEN NOTES	

RUN IN / SET UP	
SLACK / PERFORMANCE	
DAYLIGHT / LIGHTED	

RESULTS

WINNING TIME				
	1D		PAYOUT	
	2D		PAYOUT	
	3D		PAYOUT	
	4D		PAYOUT	
	5D		PAYOUT	
			PAYOUT	
			PAYOUT	
PLACES PAID OUT			NUMBER OF ENTRIES	

Rodeo Racing / Jackpot

NAME	

SANCTION / ASSOCIATION		DATE		TIME	:
LOCATION		MILES AWAY			
ENTRY FEE	$	ADDED MONEY	$		
SIDE POT Y/N TYPE		ENTRY FEE	$	ADDED MONEY	$
SIDE POT Y/N TYPE		ENTRY FEE	$	ADDED MONEY	$
TIME OUTS ALLOWED	○ YES ○ NO	STALLS AVAILABLE	○ YES ○ NO	FEE	$
ENTER: ON SITE / CALL IN DATE		TIME	:	PHONE	
BUDDY		CONFIRMATION #		CALL BACK	
DRAW					

HEALTH REQUIREMENTS

GATE		RUN IN / SET UP	
GROUND TYPE			
GROUND CONDITION			
POSITION ON THE GROUND			
WEATHER CONDITIONS			
TEMPERATURE		SLACK / PERFORMANCE	
INDOOR / OUTDOOR		DAYLIGHT / LIGHTED	
OTHER PEN NOTES			

RESULTS

WINNING TIME	ID		PAYOUT	
	2D		PAYOUT	
	3D		PAYOUT	
	4D		PAYOUT	
	5D		PAYOUT	
			PAYOUT	
			PAYOUT	
PLACES PAID OUT			NUMBER OF ENTRIES	

Rodeo Racing / Jackpot

NAME	

SANCTION / ASSOCIATION		DATE		TIME	:
LOCATION		MILES AWAY			
ENTRY FEE	$	ADDED MONEY	$		
SIDE POT Y/N TYPE		ENTRY FEE	$	ADDED MONEY	$
SIDE POT Y/N TYPE		ENTRY FEE	$	ADDED MONEY	$
TIME OUTS ALLOWED	○ YES ○ NO	STALLS AVAILABLE	○ YES ○ NO	FEE	$
ENTER: ON SITE / CALL IN DATE		TIME	:	PHONE	
BUDDY		CONFIRMATION #		CALL BACK	
DRAW					

HEALTH REQUIREMENTS

GATE		RUN IN / SET UP	
GROUND TYPE			
GROUND CONDITION			
POSITION ON THE GROUND			
WEATHER CONDITIONS			
TEMPERATURE		SLACK / PERFORMANCE	
INDOOR / OUTDOOR		DAYLIGHT / LIGHTED	
OTHER PEN NOTES			

RESULTS

WINNING TIME	1D		PAYOUT	
	2D		PAYOUT	
	3D		PAYOUT	
	4D		PAYOUT	
	5D		PAYOUT	
			PAYOUT	
			PAYOUT	
PLACES PAID OUT			NUMBER OF ENTRIES	

Rodeo Racing / Jackpot

NAME	

SANCTION / ASSOCIATION		DATE		TIME	:
LOCATION		MILES AWAY			
ENTRY FEE	$	ADDED MONEY	$		
SIDE POT Y/N TYPE		ENTRY FEE	$	ADDED MONEY	$
SIDE POT Y/N TYPE		ENTRY FEE	$	ADDED MONEY	$
TIME OUTS ALLOWED	○ YES ○ NO	STALLS AVAILABLE	○ YES ○ NO	FEE	$
ENTER: ON SITE / CALL IN DATE		TIME	:	PHONE	
BUDDY		CONFIRMATION #		CALL BACK	
DRAW					

HEALTH REQUIREMENTS

GATE		RUN IN / SET UP	
GROUND TYPE			
GROUND CONDITION			
POSITION ON THE GROUND			
WEATHER CONDITIONS			
TEMPERATURE		SLACK / PERFORMANCE	
INDOOR / OUTDOOR		DAYLIGHT / LIGHTED	
OTHER PEN NOTES			

RESULTS

WINNING TIME	ID		PAYOUT	
	2D		PAYOUT	
	3D		PAYOUT	
	4D		PAYOUT	
	5D		PAYOUT	
			PAYOUT	
			PAYOUT	
PLACES PAID OUT			NUMBER OF ENTRIES	

Rodeo Racing / Jackpot

NAME	

SANCTION / ASSOCIATION		DATE		TIME	:
LOCATION		MILES AWAY			
ENTRY FEE	$	ADDED MONEY	$		
SIDE POT Y/N TYPE		ENTRY FEE	$	ADDED MONEY	$
SIDE POT Y/N TYPE		ENTRY FEE	$	ADDED MONEY	$
TIME OUTS ALLOWED	○ YES ○ NO	STALLS AVAILABLE	○ YES ○ NO	FEE	$
ENTER: ON SITE / CALL IN DATE		TIME	:	PHONE	
BUDDY		CONFIRMATION #		CALL BACK	
DRAW					

HEALTH REQUIREMENTS	

GATE		RUN IN / SET UP	
GROUND TYPE			
GROUND CONDITION			
POSITION ON THE GROUND			
WEATHER CONDITIONS			
TEMPERATURE		SLACK / PERFORMANCE	
INDOOR / OUTDOOR		DAYLIGHT / LIGHTED	
OTHER PEN NOTES			

RESULTS

WINNING TIME	ID		PAYOUT	
	2D		PAYOUT	
	3D		PAYOUT	
	4D		PAYOUT	
	5D		PAYOUT	
			PAYOUT	
			PAYOUT	
PLACES PAID OUT			NUMBER OF ENTRIES	

Rodeo Racing / Jackpot

NAME	

SANCTION / ASSOCIATION		DATE		TIME	:
LOCATION		MILES AWAY			
ENTRY FEE	$	ADDED MONEY	$		
SIDE POT Y/N TYPE		ENTRY FEE	$	ADDED MONEY	$
SIDE POT Y/N TYPE		ENTRY FEE	$	ADDED MONEY	$
TIME OUTS ALLOWED	○ YES ○ NO	STALLS AVAILABLE	○ YES ○ NO	FEE	$
ENTER: ON SITE / CALL IN DATE		TIME	:	PHONE	
BUDDY		CONFIRMATION #		CALL BACK	
DRAW					

HEALTH REQUIREMENTS

GATE	
GROUND TYPE	
GROUND CONDITION	
POSITION ON THE GROUND	
WEATHER CONDITIONS	
TEMPERATURE	
INDOOR / OUTDOOR	
OTHER PEN NOTES	

RUN IN / SET UP	
SLACK / PERFORMANCE	
DAYLIGHT / LIGHTED	

RESULTS

WINNING TIME	ID		PAYOUT	
	2D		PAYOUT	
	3D		PAYOUT	
	4D		PAYOUT	
	5D		PAYOUT	
			PAYOUT	
			PAYOUT	
PLACES PAID OUT			NUMBER OF ENTRIES	

Rodeo Racing / Jackpot

NAME	

SANCTION / ASSOCIATION		DATE		TIME	:
LOCATION		MILES AWAY			
ENTRY FEE	$	ADDED MONEY	$		
SIDE POT Y/N TYPE		ENTRY FEE	$	ADDED MONEY	$
SIDE POT Y/N TYPE		ENTRY FEE	$	ADDED MONEY	$
TIME OUTS ALLOWED	○ YES ○ NO	STALLS AVAILABLE	○ YES ○ NO	FEE	$
ENTER: ON SITE / CALL IN DATE		TIME	:	PHONE	
BUDDY		CONFIRMATION #		CALL BACK	
DRAW					

HEALTH REQUIREMENTS

GATE		RUN IN / SET UP	
GROUND TYPE			
GROUND CONDITION			
POSITION ON THE GROUND			
WEATHER CONDITIONS			
TEMPERATURE		SLACK / PERFORMANCE	
INDOOR / OUTDOOR		DAYLIGHT / LIGHTED	
OTHER PEN NOTES			

RESULTS

WINNING TIME			PAYOUT	
	1D		PAYOUT	
	2D		PAYOUT	
	3D		PAYOUT	
	4D		PAYOUT	
	5D		PAYOUT	
			PAYOUT	
			PAYOUT	
PLACES PAID OUT			NUMBER OF ENTRIES	

Rodeo Racing / Jackpot

NAME	

SANCTION / ASSOCIATION		DATE		TIME	:
LOCATION		MILES AWAY			
ENTRY FEE	$	ADDED MONEY	$		
SIDE POT Y/N TYPE		ENTRY FEE	$	ADDED MONEY	$
SIDE POT Y/N TYPE		ENTRY FEE	$	ADDED MONEY	$
TIME OUTS ALLOWED	○ YES ○ NO	STALLS AVAILABLE	○ YES ○ NO	FEE	$
ENTER: ON SITE / CALL IN DATE		TIME	:	PHONE	
BUDDY		CONFIRMATION #		CALL BACK	
DRAW					

HEALTH REQUIREMENTS

GATE		RUN IN / SET UP	
GROUND TYPE			
GROUND CONDITION			
POSITION ON THE GROUND			
WEATHER CONDITIONS			
TEMPERATURE		SLACK / PERFORMANCE	
INDOOR / OUTDOOR		DAYLIGHT / LIGHTED	
OTHER PEN NOTES			

RESULTS

WINNING TIME	ID		PAYOUT	
	2D		PAYOUT	
	3D		PAYOUT	
	4D		PAYOUT	
	5D		PAYOUT	
			PAYOUT	
			PAYOUT	
PLACES PAID OUT			NUMBER OF ENTRIES	

Rodeo Racing / Jackpot

NAME	

SANCTION / ASSOCIATION		DATE		TIME	:
LOCATION		MILES AWAY			
ENTRY FEE	$	ADDED MONEY	$		
SIDE POT Y/N TYPE		ENTRY FEE	$	ADDED MONEY	$
SIDE POT Y/N TYPE		ENTRY FEE	$	ADDED MONEY	$
TIME OUTS ALLOWED	○ YES ○ NO	STALLS AVAILABLE	○ YES ○ NO	FEE	$
ENTER: ON SITE / CALL IN DATE		TIME	:	PHONE	
BUDDY		CONFIRMATION #		CALL BACK	
DRAW					

HEALTH REQUIREMENTS

GATE		RUN IN / SET UP	
GROUND TYPE			
GROUND CONDITION			
POSITION ON THE GROUND			
WEATHER CONDITIONS			
TEMPERATURE		SLACK / PERFORMANCE	
INDOOR / OUTDOOR		DAYLIGHT / LIGHTED	
OTHER PEN NOTES			

RESULTS

WINNING TIME	ID		PAYOUT	
	2D		PAYOUT	
	3D		PAYOUT	
	4D		PAYOUT	
	5D		PAYOUT	
			PAYOUT	
			PAYOUT	
PLACES PAID OUT			NUMBER OF ENTRIES	

Rodeo Racing / Jackpot

NAME	

SANCTION / ASSOCIATION		DATE		TIME	:
LOCATION		MILES AWAY			
ENTRY FEE	$	ADDED MONEY	$		
SIDE POT Y/N TYPE		ENTRY FEE	$	ADDED MONEY	$
SIDE POT Y/N TYPE		ENTRY FEE	$	ADDED MONEY	$
TIME OUTS ALLOWED	○ YES ○ NO	STALLS AVAILABLE	○ YES ○ NO	FEE	$
ENTER: ON SITE / CALL IN DATE		TIME	:	PHONE	
BUDDY		CONFIRMATION #		CALL BACK	
DRAW					

HEALTH REQUIREMENTS

GATE		RUN IN / SET UP	
GROUND TYPE			
GROUND CONDITION			
POSITION ON THE GROUND			
WEATHER CONDITIONS			
TEMPERATURE		SLACK / PERFORMANCE	
INDOOR / OUTDOOR		DAYLIGHT / LIGHTED	
OTHER PEN NOTES			

RESULTS

WINNING TIME	ID		PAYOUT	
	2D		PAYOUT	
	3D		PAYOUT	
	4D		PAYOUT	
	5D		PAYOUT	
			PAYOUT	
			PAYOUT	
PLACES PAID OUT			NUMBER OF ENTRIES	

Rodeo Racing / Jackpot

NAME					
SANCTION / ASSOCIATION		DATE		TIME	:
LOCATION		MILES AWAY			
ENTRY FEE	$	ADDED MONEY	$		
SIDE POT Y/N TYPE		ENTRY FEE	$	ADDED MONEY	$
SIDE POT Y/N TYPE		ENTRY FEE	$	ADDED MONEY	$
TIME OUTS ALLOWED	○ YES ○ NO	STALLS AVAILABLE	○ YES ○ NO	FEE	$
ENTER: ON SITE / CALL IN DATE		TIME	:	PHONE	
BUDDY		CONFIRMATION #		CALL BACK	
DRAW					

HEALTH REQUIREMENTS	

GATE		RUN IN / SET UP	
GROUND TYPE			
GROUND CONDITION			
POSITION ON THE GROUND			
WEATHER CONDITIONS			
TEMPERATURE		SLACK / PERFORMANCE	
INDOOR / OUTDOOR		DAYLIGHT / LIGHTED	
OTHER PEN NOTES			

RESULTS

WINNING TIME			PAYOUT	
	1D		PAYOUT	
	2D		PAYOUT	
	3D		PAYOUT	
	4D		PAYOUT	
	5D		PAYOUT	
			PAYOUT	
			PAYOUT	
PLACES PAID OUT			NUMBER OF ENTRIES	

Rodeo Racing / Jackpot

NAME	

SANCTION / ASSOCIATION		DATE		TIME	:
LOCATION		MILES AWAY			
ENTRY FEE	$	ADDED MONEY	$		
SIDE POT Y/N TYPE		ENTRY FEE	$	ADDED MONEY	$
SIDE POT Y/N TYPE		ENTRY FEE	$	ADDED MONEY	$
TIME OUTS ALLOWED	○ YES ○ NO	STALLS AVAILABLE	○ YES ○ NO	FEE	$
ENTER: ON SITE / CALL IN DATE		TIME	:	PHONE	
BUDDY		CONFIRMATION #		CALL BACK	
DRAW					

HEALTH REQUIREMENTS

GATE		RUN IN / SET UP	
GROUND TYPE			
GROUND CONDITION			
POSITION ON THE GROUND			
WEATHER CONDITIONS			
TEMPERATURE		SLACK / PERFORMANCE	
INDOOR / OUTDOOR		DAYLIGHT / LIGHTED	
OTHER PEN NOTES			

RESULTS

WINNING TIME	ID		PAYOUT	
	2D		PAYOUT	
	3D		PAYOUT	
	4D		PAYOUT	
	5D		PAYOUT	
			PAYOUT	
			PAYOUT	
PLACES PAID OUT			NUMBER OF ENTRIES	

Rodeo Racing / Jackpot

NAME	

SANCTION / ASSOCIATION		DATE		TIME	:
LOCATION		MILES AWAY			
ENTRY FEE	$	ADDED MONEY	$		
SIDE POT Y/N TYPE		ENTRY FEE	$	ADDED MONEY	$
SIDE POT Y/N TYPE		ENTRY FEE	$	ADDED MONEY	$
TIME OUTS ALLOWED	○ YES ○ NO	STALLS AVAILABLE	○ YES ○ NO	FEE	$
ENTER: ON SITE / CALL IN DATE		TIME	:	PHONE	
BUDDY		CONFIRMATION #		CALL BACK	
DRAW					

HEALTH REQUIREMENTS	

GATE		RUN IN / SET UP	
GROUND TYPE			
GROUND CONDITION			
POSITION ON THE GROUND			
WEATHER CONDITIONS			
TEMPERATURE		SLACK / PERFORMANCE	
INDOOR / OUTDOOR		DAYLIGHT / LIGHTED	
OTHER PEN NOTES			

RESULTS

WINNING TIME	ID		PAYOUT	
	2D		PAYOUT	
	3D		PAYOUT	
	4D		PAYOUT	
	5D		PAYOUT	
			PAYOUT	
			PAYOUT	
PLACES PAID OUT			NUMBER OF ENTRIES	

Rodeo Racing / Jackpot

NAME	

SANCTION / ASSOCIATION		DATE		TIME	:
LOCATION		MILES AWAY			
ENTRY FEE	$	ADDED MONEY	$		
SIDE POT Y/N TYPE		ENTRY FEE	$	ADDED MONEY	$
SIDE POT Y/N TYPE		ENTRY FEE	$	ADDED MONEY	$
TIME OUTS ALLOWED	○ YES ○ NO	STALLS AVAILABLE	○ YES ○ NO	FEE	$
ENTER: ON SITE / CALL IN DATE		TIME	:	PHONE	
BUDDY		CONFIRMATION #		CALL BACK	
DRAW					

HEALTH REQUIREMENTS

GATE		RUN IN / SET UP	
GROUND TYPE			
GROUND CONDITION			
POSITION ON THE GROUND			
WEATHER CONDITIONS			
TEMPERATURE		SLACK / PERFORMANCE	
INDOOR / OUTDOOR		DAYLIGHT / LIGHTED	
OTHER PEN NOTES			

RESULTS

WINNING TIME	ID		PAYOUT	
	2D		PAYOUT	
	3D		PAYOUT	
	4D		PAYOUT	
	5D		PAYOUT	
			PAYOUT	
			PAYOUT	
PLACES PAID OUT			NUMBER OF ENTRIES	

Rodeo Racing / Jackpot

NAME	

SANCTION / ASSOCIATION		DATE		TIME	
LOCATION		MILES AWAY			
ENTRY FEE	$	ADDED MONEY	$		
SIDE POT Y/N TYPE		ENTRY FEE	$	ADDED MONEY	$
SIDE POT Y/N TYPE		ENTRY FEE	$	ADDED MONEY	$
TIME OUTS ALLOWED	○ YES ○ NO	STALLS AVAILABLE	○ YES ○ NO	FEE	$
ENTER: ON SITE / CALL IN DATE		TIME	:	PHONE	
BUDDY		CONFIRMATION #		CALL BACK	
DRAW					

HEALTH REQUIREMENTS

GATE		RUN IN / SET UP	
GROUND TYPE			
GROUND CONDITION			
POSITION ON THE GROUND			
WEATHER CONDITIONS			
TEMPERATURE		SLACK / PERFORMANCE	
INDOOR / OUTDOOR		DAYLIGHT / LIGHTED	
OTHER PEN NOTES			

RESULTS

WINNING TIME	1D		PAYOUT	
	2D		PAYOUT	
	3D		PAYOUT	
	4D		PAYOUT	
	5D		PAYOUT	
			PAYOUT	
			PAYOUT	

PLACES PAID OUT		NUMBER OF ENTRIES	

Rodeo Racing / Jackpot

NAME	

SANCTION / ASSOCIATION		DATE		TIME	:
LOCATION		MILES AWAY			
ENTRY FEE	$	ADDED MONEY	$		
SIDE POT Y/N TYPE		ENTRY FEE	$	ADDED MONEY	$
SIDE POT Y/N TYPE		ENTRY FEE	$	ADDED MONEY	$
TIME OUTS ALLOWED	○ YES ○ NO	STALLS AVAILABLE	○ YES ○ NO	FEE	$
ENTER: ON SITE / CALL IN DATE		TIME	:	PHONE	
BUDDY		CONFIRMATION #		CALL BACK	
DRAW					

HEALTH REQUIREMENTS

GATE		RUN IN / SET UP	
GROUND TYPE			
GROUND CONDITION			
POSITION ON THE GROUND			
WEATHER CONDITIONS			
TEMPERATURE		SLACK / PERFORMANCE	
INDOOR / OUTDOOR		DAYLIGHT / LIGHTED	
OTHER PEN NOTES			

RESULTS

WINNING TIME	ID		PAYOUT	
	2D		PAYOUT	
	3D		PAYOUT	
	4D		PAYOUT	
	5D		PAYOUT	
			PAYOUT	
			PAYOUT	
PLACES PAID OUT			NUMBER OF ENTRIES	

Rodeo Racing / Jackpot

NAME	

SANCTION / ASSOCIATION		DATE		TIME	:
LOCATION		MILES AWAY			
ENTRY FEE	$	ADDED MONEY	$		
SIDE POT Y/N TYPE		ENTRY FEE	$	ADDED MONEY	$
SIDE POT Y/N TYPE		ENTRY FEE	$	ADDED MONEY	$
TIME OUTS ALLOWED	○ YES ○ NO	STALLS AVAILABLE	○ YES ○ NO	FEE	$
ENTER: ON SITE / CALL IN DATE		TIME	:	PHONE	
BUDDY		CONFIRMATION #		CALL BACK	
DRAW					

HEALTH REQUIREMENTS	

GATE		RUN IN / SET UP	
GROUND TYPE			
GROUND CONDITION			
POSITION ON THE GROUND			
WEATHER CONDITIONS			
TEMPERATURE		SLACK / PERFORMANCE	
INDOOR / OUTDOOR		DAYLIGHT / LIGHTED	
OTHER PEN NOTES			

RESULTS					
WINNING TIME	1D		PAYOUT		
	2D		PAYOUT		
	3D		PAYOUT		
	4D		PAYOUT		
	5D		PAYOUT		
			PAYOUT		
			PAYOUT		
PLACES PAID OUT			NUMBER OF ENTRIES		

Rodeo Racing / Jackpot

NAME	

SANCTION / ASSOCIATION		DATE		TIME	:
LOCATION		MILES AWAY			
ENTRY FEE	$	ADDED MONEY	$		
SIDE POT Y/N TYPE		ENTRY FEE	$	ADDED MONEY	$
SIDE POT Y/N TYPE		ENTRY FEE	$	ADDED MONEY	$
TIME OUTS ALLOWED	○ YES ○ NO	STALLS AVAILABLE	○ YES ○ NO	FEE	$
ENTER: ON SITE / CALL IN DATE		TIME	:	PHONE	
BUDDY		CONFIRMATION #		CALL BACK	
DRAW					

HEALTH REQUIREMENTS

GATE		RUN IN / SET UP	
GROUND TYPE			
GROUND CONDITION			
POSITION ON THE GROUND			
WEATHER CONDITIONS			
TEMPERATURE		SLACK / PERFORMANCE	
INDOOR / OUTDOOR		DAYLIGHT / LIGHTED	
OTHER PEN NOTES			

RESULTS

WINNING TIME	ID		PAYOUT	
	2D		PAYOUT	
	3D		PAYOUT	
	4D		PAYOUT	
	5D		PAYOUT	
			PAYOUT	
			PAYOUT	
PLACES PAID OUT			NUMBER OF ENTRIES	

Rodeo Racing / Jackpot

NAME	

SANCTION / ASSOCIATION		DATE		TIME	:
LOCATION		MILES AWAY			
ENTRY FEE	$	ADDED MONEY	$		
SIDE POT Y/N TYPE		ENTRY FEE	$	ADDED MONEY	$
SIDE POT Y/N TYPE		ENTRY FEE	$	ADDED MONEY	$
TIME OUTS ALLOWED	○ YES ○ NO	STALLS AVAILABLE	○ YES ○ NO	FEE	$
ENTER: ON SITE / CALL IN DATE		TIME	:	PHONE	
BUDDY		CONFIRMATION #		CALL BACK	
DRAW					

HEALTH REQUIREMENTS

GATE		RUN IN / SET UP	
GROUND TYPE			
GROUND CONDITION			
POSITION ON THE GROUND			
WEATHER CONDITIONS			
TEMPERATURE		SLACK / PERFORMANCE	
INDOOR / OUTDOOR		DAYLIGHT / LIGHTED	
OTHER PEN NOTES			

RESULTS

WINNING TIME	1D		PAYOUT	
	2D		PAYOUT	
	3D		PAYOUT	
	4D		PAYOUT	
	5D		PAYOUT	
			PAYOUT	
			PAYOUT	
PLACES PAID OUT			NUMBER OF ENTRIES	

Rodeo Racing / Jackpot

NAME	

SANCTION / ASSOCIATION		DATE		TIME	:
LOCATION		MILES AWAY			
ENTRY FEE	$	ADDED MONEY	$		
SIDE POT Y/N TYPE		ENTRY FEE	$	ADDED MONEY	$
SIDE POT Y/N TYPE		ENTRY FEE	$	ADDED MONEY	$
TIME OUTS ALLOWED	○ YES ○ NO	STALLS AVAILABLE	○ YES ○ NO	FEE	$
ENTER: ON SITE / CALL IN DATE		TIME	:	PHONE	
BUDDY		CONFIRMATION #		CALL BACK	
DRAW					

HEALTH REQUIREMENTS

GATE		RUN IN / SET UP	
GROUND TYPE			
GROUND CONDITION			
POSITION ON THE GROUND			
WEATHER CONDITIONS			
TEMPERATURE		SLACK / PERFORMANCE	
INDOOR / OUTDOOR		DAYLIGHT / LIGHTED	
OTHER PEN NOTES			

RESULTS

WINNING TIME	ID		PAYOUT	
	2D		PAYOUT	
	3D		PAYOUT	
	4D		PAYOUT	
	5D		PAYOUT	
			PAYOUT	
			PAYOUT	
PLACES PAID OUT			NUMBER OF ENTRIES	

Rodeo Racing / Jackpot

NAME	

SANCTION / ASSOCIATION		DATE		TIME		:
LOCATION		MILES AWAY				
ENTRY FEE	$	ADDED MONEY	$			
SIDE POT Y/N TYPE		ENTRY FEE	$	ADDED MONEY	$	
SIDE POT Y/N TYPE		ENTRY FEE	$	ADDED MONEY	$	
TIME OUTS ALLOWED	○ YES ○ NO	STALLS AVAILABLE	○ YES ○ NO	FEE	$	
ENTER: ON SITE / CALL IN DATE		TIME	:	PHONE		
BUDDY		CONFIRMATION #		CALL BACK		
DRAW						

HEALTH REQUIREMENTS

GATE		RUN IN / SET UP	
GROUND TYPE			
GROUND CONDITION			
POSITION ON THE GROUND			
WEATHER CONDITIONS			
TEMPERATURE		SLACK / PERFORMANCE	
INDOOR / OUTDOOR		DAYLIGHT / LIGHTED	
OTHER PEN NOTES			

RESULTS

WINNING TIME				
	1D		PAYOUT	
	2D		PAYOUT	
	3D		PAYOUT	
	4D		PAYOUT	
	5D		PAYOUT	
			PAYOUT	
			PAYOUT	
PLACES PAID OUT			NUMBER OF ENTRIES	

Rodeo Racing / Jackpot

NAME	

SANCTION / ASSOCIATION		DATE		TIME	:
LOCATION		MILES AWAY			
ENTRY FEE	$	ADDED MONEY	$		
SIDE POT Y/N TYPE		ENTRY FEE	$	ADDED MONEY	$
SIDE POT Y/N TYPE		ENTRY FEE	$	ADDED MONEY	$
TIME OUTS ALLOWED	○ YES ○ NO	STALLS AVAILABLE	○ YES ○ NO	FEE	$
ENTER: ON SITE / CALL IN DATE		TIME	:	PHONE	
BUDDY		CONFIRMATION #		CALL BACK	
DRAW					

HEALTH REQUIREMENTS

GATE		RUN IN / SET UP	
GROUND TYPE			
GROUND CONDITION			
POSITION ON THE GROUND			
WEATHER CONDITIONS			
TEMPERATURE		SLACK / PERFORMANCE	
INDOOR / OUTDOOR		DAYLIGHT / LIGHTED	
OTHER PEN NOTES			

RESULTS

WINNING TIME	1D		PAYOUT	
	2D		PAYOUT	
	3D		PAYOUT	
	4D		PAYOUT	
	5D		PAYOUT	
			PAYOUT	
			PAYOUT	
PLACES PAID OUT			NUMBER OF ENTRIES	

Rodeo Racing / Jackpot

NAME					
SANCTION / ASSOCIATION		DATE		TIME	:
LOCATION		MILES AWAY			
ENTRY FEE	$	ADDED MONEY	$		
SIDE POT Y/N TYPE		ENTRY FEE	$	ADDED MONEY	$
SIDE POT Y/N TYPE		ENTRY FEE	$	ADDED MONEY	$
TIME OUTS ALLOWED	○ YES ○ NO	STALLS AVAILABLE	○ YES ○ NO	FEE	$
ENTER: ON SITE / CALL IN DATE		TIME	:	PHONE	
BUDDY		CONFIRMATION #		CALL BACK	
DRAW					

HEALTH REQUIREMENTS

GATE		RUN IN / SET UP	
GROUND TYPE			
GROUND CONDITION			
POSITION ON THE GROUND			
WEATHER CONDITIONS			
TEMPERATURE		SLACK / PERFORMANCE	
INDOOR / OUTDOOR		DAYLIGHT / LIGHTED	
OTHER PEN NOTES			

RESULTS

WINNING TIME	1D		PAYOUT	
	2D		PAYOUT	
	3D		PAYOUT	
	4D		PAYOUT	
	5D		PAYOUT	
			PAYOUT	
			PAYOUT	
PLACES PAID OUT			NUMBER OF ENTRIES	

Rodeo Racing / Jackpot

NAME	

SANCTION / ASSOCIATION		DATE		TIME	:
LOCATION		MILES AWAY			
ENTRY FEE	$	ADDED MONEY	$		
SIDE POT Y/N TYPE		ENTRY FEE	$	ADDED MONEY	$
SIDE POT Y/N TYPE		ENTRY FEE	$	ADDED MONEY	$
TIME OUTS ALLOWED	○ YES ○ NO	STALLS AVAILABLE	○ YES ○ NO	FEE	$
ENTER: ON SITE / CALL IN DATE		TIME	:	PHONE	
BUDDY		CONFIRMATION #		CALL BACK	
DRAW					

HEALTH REQUIREMENTS

GATE		RUN IN / SET UP	
GROUND TYPE			
GROUND CONDITION			
POSITION ON THE GROUND			
WEATHER CONDITIONS			
TEMPERATURE		SLACK / PERFORMANCE	
INDOOR / OUTDOOR		DAYLIGHT / LIGHTED	
OTHER PEN NOTES			

RESULTS

WINNING TIME	ID		PAYOUT	
	2D		PAYOUT	
	3D		PAYOUT	
	4D		PAYOUT	
	5D		PAYOUT	
			PAYOUT	
			PAYOUT	
PLACES PAID OUT			NUMBER OF ENTRIES	

Rodeo Racing / Jackpot

NAME	

SANCTION / ASSOCIATION		DATE		TIME	:
LOCATION		MILES AWAY			
ENTRY FEE	$	ADDED MONEY	$		
SIDE POT Y/N TYPE		ENTRY FEE	$	ADDED MONEY	$
SIDE POT Y/N TYPE		ENTRY FEE	$	ADDED MONEY	$
TIME OUTS ALLOWED	○ YES ○ NO	STALLS AVAILABLE	○ YES ○ NO	FEE	$
ENTER: ON SITE / CALL IN DATE		TIME	:	PHONE	
BUDDY		CONFIRMATION #		CALL BACK	
DRAW					

HEALTH REQUIREMENTS

GATE		RUN IN / SET UP	
GROUND TYPE			
GROUND CONDITION			
POSITION ON THE GROUND			
WEATHER CONDITIONS			
TEMPERATURE		SLACK / PERFORMANCE	
INDOOR / OUTDOOR		DAYLIGHT / LIGHTED	
OTHER PEN NOTES			

RESULTS

WINNING TIME	ID		PAYOUT	
	2D		PAYOUT	
	3D		PAYOUT	
	4D		PAYOUT	
	5D		PAYOUT	
			PAYOUT	
			PAYOUT	
PLACES PAID OUT			NUMBER OF ENTRIES	

Rodeo Racing / Jackpot

NAME	

SANCTION / ASSOCIATION		DATE		TIME	:
LOCATION		MILES AWAY			
ENTRY FEE	$	ADDED MONEY	$		
SIDE POT Y/N TYPE		ENTRY FEE	$	ADDED MONEY	$
SIDE POT Y/N TYPE		ENTRY FEE	$	ADDED MONEY	$
TIME OUTS ALLOWED	○ YES ○ NO	STALLS AVAILABLE	○ YES ○ NO	FEE	$
ENTER: ON SITE / CALL IN DATE		TIME	:	PHONE	
BUDDY		CONFIRMATION #		CALL BACK	
DRAW					

HEALTH REQUIREMENTS

GATE		RUN IN / SET UP	
GROUND TYPE			
GROUND CONDITION			
POSITION ON THE GROUND			
WEATHER CONDITIONS			
TEMPERATURE		SLACK / PERFORMANCE	
INDOOR / OUTDOOR		DAYLIGHT / LIGHTED	
OTHER PEN NOTES			

RESULTS

WINNING TIME	1D		PAYOUT	
	2D		PAYOUT	
	3D		PAYOUT	
	4D		PAYOUT	
	5D		PAYOUT	
			PAYOUT	
			PAYOUT	
PLACES PAID OUT			NUMBER OF ENTRIES	

Rodeo Racing / Jackpot

NAME					
SANCTION / ASSOCIATION		DATE		TIME	:
LOCATION		MILES AWAY			
ENTRY FEE	$	ADDED MONEY	$		
SIDE POT Y/N TYPE		ENTRY FEE	$	ADDED MONEY	$
SIDE POT Y/N TYPE		ENTRY FEE	$	ADDED MONEY	$
TIME OUTS ALLOWED	○ YES ○ NO	STALLS AVAILABLE	○ YES ○ NO	FEE	$
ENTER: ON SITE / CALL IN DATE		TIME	:	PHONE	
BUDDY		CONFIRMATION #		CALL BACK	
DRAW					

HEALTH REQUIREMENTS

GATE		RUN IN / SET UP	
GROUND TYPE			
GROUND CONDITION			
POSITION ON THE GROUND			
WEATHER CONDITIONS			
TEMPERATURE		SLACK / PERFORMANCE	
INDOOR / OUTDOOR		DAYLIGHT / LIGHTED	
OTHER PEN NOTES			

RESULTS

WINNING TIME			PAYOUT	
	1D		PAYOUT	
	2D		PAYOUT	
	3D		PAYOUT	
	4D		PAYOUT	
	5D		PAYOUT	
			PAYOUT	
			PAYOUT	
PLACES PAID OUT			NUMBER OF ENTRIES	

Rodeo Racing / Jackpot

NAME	

SANCTION / ASSOCIATION		DATE		TIME	:
LOCATION		MILES AWAY			
ENTRY FEE	$	ADDED MONEY	$		
SIDE POT Y/N TYPE		ENTRY FEE	$	ADDED MONEY	$
SIDE POT Y/N TYPE		ENTRY FEE	$	ADDED MONEY	$
TIME OUTS ALLOWED	○ YES ○ NO	STALLS AVAILABLE	○ YES ○ NO	FEE	$
ENTER: ON SITE / CALL IN DATE		TIME	:	PHONE	
BUDDY		CONFIRMATION #		CALL BACK	
DRAW					

HEALTH REQUIREMENTS

GATE		RUN IN / SET UP	
GROUND TYPE			
GROUND CONDITION			
POSITION ON THE GROUND			
WEATHER CONDITIONS			
TEMPERATURE		SLACK / PERFORMANCE	
INDOOR / OUTDOOR		DAYLIGHT / LIGHTED	
OTHER PEN NOTES			

RESULTS

WINNING TIME	ID		PAYOUT	
	2D		PAYOUT	
	3D		PAYOUT	
	4D		PAYOUT	
	5D		PAYOUT	
			PAYOUT	
			PAYOUT	
PLACES PAID OUT			NUMBER OF ENTRIES	

Rodeo Racing / Jackpot

NAME	

SANCTION / ASSOCIATION		DATE		TIME		:
LOCATION		MILES AWAY				
ENTRY FEE	$	ADDED MONEY	$			
SIDE POT Y/N TYPE		ENTRY FEE	$	ADDED MONEY	$	
SIDE POT Y/N TYPE		ENTRY FEE	$	ADDED MONEY	$	
TIME OUTS ALLOWED	○ YES ○ NO	STALLS AVAILABLE	○ YES ○ NO	FEE	$	
ENTER: ON SITE / CALL IN DATE		TIME	:	PHONE		
BUDDY		CONFIRMATION #		CALL BACK		
DRAW						

HEALTH REQUIREMENTS

GATE		RUN IN / SET UP	
GROUND TYPE			
GROUND CONDITION			
POSITION ON THE GROUND			
WEATHER CONDITIONS			
TEMPERATURE		SLACK / PERFORMANCE	
INDOOR / OUTDOOR		DAYLIGHT / LIGHTED	
OTHER PEN NOTES			

RESULTS

WINNING TIME	ID		PAYOUT	
	1D		PAYOUT	
	2D		PAYOUT	
	3D		PAYOUT	
	4D		PAYOUT	
	5D		PAYOUT	
			PAYOUT	
			PAYOUT	
PLACES PAID OUT			NUMBER OF ENTRIES	

Rodeo Racing / Jackpot

NAME	

SANCTION / ASSOCIATION		DATE		TIME	:
LOCATION		MILES AWAY			
ENTRY FEE	$	ADDED MONEY	$		
SIDE POT Y/N TYPE		ENTRY FEE	$	ADDED MONEY	$
SIDE POT Y/N TYPE		ENTRY FEE	$	ADDED MONEY	$
TIME OUTS ALLOWED	○ YES ○ NO	STALLS AVAILABLE	○ YES ○ NO	FEE	$
ENTER: ON SITE / CALL IN DATE		TIME	:	PHONE	
BUDDY		CONFIRMATION #		CALL BACK	
DRAW					

HEALTH REQUIREMENTS

GATE		RUN IN / SET UP	
GROUND TYPE			
GROUND CONDITION			
POSITION ON THE GROUND			
WEATHER CONDITIONS			
TEMPERATURE		SLACK / PERFORMANCE	
INDOOR / OUTDOOR		DAYLIGHT / LIGHTED	
OTHER PEN NOTES			

RESULTS

WINNING TIME	ID		PAYOUT	
	2D		PAYOUT	
	3D		PAYOUT	
	4D		PAYOUT	
	5D		PAYOUT	
			PAYOUT	
			PAYOUT	
PLACES PAID OUT			NUMBER OF ENTRIES	

Rodeo Racing / Jackpot

NAME	

SANCTION / ASSOCIATION		DATE		TIME	:
LOCATION		MILES AWAY			
ENTRY FEE	$	ADDED MONEY	$		
SIDE POT Y/N TYPE		ENTRY FEE	$	ADDED MONEY	$
SIDE POT Y/N TYPE		ENTRY FEE	$	ADDED MONEY	$
TIME OUTS ALLOWED	○ YES ○ NO	STALLS AVAILABLE	○ YES ○ NO	FEE	$
ENTER: ON SITE / CALL IN DATE		TIME	:	PHONE	
BUDDY		CONFIRMATION #		CALL BACK	
DRAW					

HEALTH REQUIREMENTS

GATE		RUN IN / SET UP	
GROUND TYPE			
GROUND CONDITION			
POSITION ON THE GROUND			
WEATHER CONDITIONS			
TEMPERATURE		SLACK / PERFORMANCE	
INDOOR / OUTDOOR		DAYLIGHT / LIGHTED	
OTHER PEN NOTES			

RESULTS				
WINNING TIME	1D		PAYOUT	
	2D		PAYOUT	
	3D		PAYOUT	
	4D		PAYOUT	
	5D		PAYOUT	
			PAYOUT	
			PAYOUT	
PLACES PAID OUT			NUMBER OF ENTRIES	

Rodeo Racing / Jackpot

NAME	

SANCTION / ASSOCIATION		DATE		TIME	:
LOCATION		MILES AWAY			
ENTRY FEE	$	ADDED MONEY	$		
SIDE POT Y/N TYPE		ENTRY FEE	$	ADDED MONEY	$
SIDE POT Y/N TYPE		ENTRY FEE	$	ADDED MONEY	$
TIME OUTS ALLOWED	○ YES ○ NO	STALLS AVAILABLE	○ YES ○ NO	FEE	$
ENTER: ON SITE / CALL IN DATE		TIME	:	PHONE	
BUDDY		CONFIRMATION #		CALL BACK	
DRAW					

HEALTH REQUIREMENTS

GATE		RUN IN / SET UP	
GROUND TYPE			
GROUND CONDITION			
POSITION ON THE GROUND			
WEATHER CONDITIONS			
TEMPERATURE		SLACK / PERFORMANCE	
INDOOR / OUTDOOR		DAYLIGHT / LIGHTED	
OTHER PEN NOTES			

RESULTS

WINNING TIME	ID		PAYOUT	
	2D		PAYOUT	
	3D		PAYOUT	
	4D		PAYOUT	
	5D		PAYOUT	
			PAYOUT	
			PAYOUT	
PLACES PAID OUT			NUMBER OF ENTRIES	

Rodeo Racing / Jackpot

NAME	

SANCTION / ASSOCIATION		DATE		TIME	:
LOCATION		MILES AWAY			
ENTRY FEE	$	ADDED MONEY	$		
SIDE POT Y/N TYPE		ENTRY FEE	$	ADDED MONEY	$
SIDE POT Y/N TYPE		ENTRY FEE	$	ADDED MONEY	$
TIME OUTS ALLOWED	○ YES ○ NO	STALLS AVAILABLE	○ YES ○ NO	FEE	$
ENTER: ON SITE / CALL IN DATE		TIME	:	PHONE	
BUDDY		CONFIRMATION #		CALL BACK	
DRAW					

HEALTH REQUIREMENTS

GATE		RUN IN / SET UP	
GROUND TYPE			
GROUND CONDITION			
POSITION ON THE GROUND			
WEATHER CONDITIONS			
TEMPERATURE		SLACK / PERFORMANCE	
INDOOR / OUTDOOR		DAYLIGHT / LIGHTED	
OTHER PEN NOTES			

RESULTS				
WINNING TIME	1D		PAYOUT	
	2D		PAYOUT	
	3D		PAYOUT	
	4D		PAYOUT	
	5D		PAYOUT	
			PAYOUT	
			PAYOUT	
PLACES PAID OUT			NUMBER OF ENTRIES	

Rodeo Racing / Jackpot

NAME	

SANCTION / ASSOCIATION		DATE		TIME	:
LOCATION		MILES AWAY			
ENTRY FEE	$	ADDED MONEY	$		
SIDE POT Y/N TYPE		ENTRY FEE	$	ADDED MONEY	$
SIDE POT Y/N TYPE		ENTRY FEE	$	ADDED MONEY	$
TIME OUTS ALLOWED	○ YES ○ NO	STALLS AVAILABLE	○ YES ○ NO	FEE	$
ENTER: ON SITE / CALL IN DATE		TIME	:	PHONE	
BUDDY		CONFIRMATION #		CALL BACK	
DRAW					

HEALTH REQUIREMENTS

GATE		RUN IN / SET UP	
GROUND TYPE			
GROUND CONDITION			
POSITION ON THE GROUND			
WEATHER CONDITIONS			
TEMPERATURE		SLACK / PERFORMANCE	
INDOOR / OUTDOOR		DAYLIGHT / LIGHTED	
OTHER PEN NOTES			

RESULTS

WINNING TIME	ID		PAYOUT	
	2D		PAYOUT	
	3D		PAYOUT	
	4D		PAYOUT	
	5D		PAYOUT	
			PAYOUT	
			PAYOUT	
PLACES PAID OUT			NUMBER OF ENTRIES	

Rodeo Racing / Jackpot

NAME	

SANCTION / ASSOCIATION		DATE		TIME	:
LOCATION		MILES AWAY			
ENTRY FEE	$	ADDED MONEY	$		
SIDE POT Y/N TYPE		ENTRY FEE	$	ADDED MONEY	$
SIDE POT Y/N TYPE		ENTRY FEE	$	ADDED MONEY	$
TIME OUTS ALLOWED	○ YES ○ NO	STALLS AVAILABLE	○ YES ○ NO	FEE	$
ENTER: ON SITE / CALL IN DATE		TIME	:	PHONE	
BUDDY		CONFIRMATION #		CALL BACK	
DRAW					

HEALTH REQUIREMENTS

GATE	
GROUND TYPE	
GROUND CONDITION	
POSITION ON THE GROUND	
WEATHER CONDITIONS	
TEMPERATURE	
INDOOR / OUTDOOR	
OTHER PEN NOTES	

RUN IN / SET UP	
SLACK / PERFORMANCE	
DAYLIGHT / LIGHTED	

RESULTS

WINNING TIME	ID		PAYOUT	
	1）		PAYOUT	
	2）		PAYOUT	
	3）		PAYOUT	
	4）		PAYOUT	
	5）		PAYOUT	
			PAYOUT	
			PAYOUT	
PLACES PAID OUT			NUMBER OF ENTRIES	

Rodeo Racing / Jackpot

NAME	

SANCTION / ASSOCIATION		DATE		TIME	:
LOCATION		MILES AWAY			
ENTRY FEE	$	ADDED MONEY	$		
SIDE POT Y/N TYPE		ENTRY FEE	$	ADDED MONEY	$
SIDE POT Y/N TYPE		ENTRY FEE	$	ADDED MONEY	$
TIME OUTS ALLOWED	○ YES ○ NO	STALLS AVAILABLE	○ YES ○ NO	FEE	$
ENTER: ON SITE / CALL IN DATE		TIME	:	PHONE	
BUDDY		CONFIRMATION #		CALL BACK	
DRAW					

HEALTH REQUIREMENTS

GATE		RUN IN / SET UP	
GROUND TYPE			
GROUND CONDITION			
POSITION ON THE GROUND			
WEATHER CONDITIONS			
TEMPERATURE		SLACK / PERFORMANCE	
INDOOR / OUTDOOR		DAYLIGHT / LIGHTED	
OTHER PEN NOTES			

RESULTS

WINNING TIME	ID		PAYOUT	
	2D		PAYOUT	
	3D		PAYOUT	
	4D		PAYOUT	
	5D		PAYOUT	
			PAYOUT	
			PAYOUT	
PLACES PAID OUT			NUMBER OF ENTRIES	

Rodeo Racing / Jackpot

NAME	

SANCTION / ASSOCIATION		DATE		TIME	:
LOCATION		MILES AWAY			
ENTRY FEE	$	ADDED MONEY	$		
SIDE POT Y/N TYPE		ENTRY FEE	$	ADDED MONEY	$
SIDE POT Y/N TYPE		ENTRY FEE	$	ADDED MONEY	$
TIME OUTS ALLOWED	○ YES ○ NO	STALLS AVAILABLE	○ YES ○ NO	FEE	$
ENTER: ON SITE / CALL IN DATE		TIME	:	PHONE	
BUDDY		CONFIRMATION #		CALL BACK	
DRAW					

HEALTH REQUIREMENTS

GATE		RUN IN / SET UP	
GROUND TYPE			
GROUND CONDITION			
POSITION ON THE GROUND			
WEATHER CONDITIONS			
TEMPERATURE		SLACK / PERFORMANCE	
INDOOR / OUTDOOR		DAYLIGHT / LIGHTED	
OTHER PEN NOTES			

RESULTS				
WINNING TIME	1D		PAYOUT	
	2D		PAYOUT	
	3D		PAYOUT	
	4D		PAYOUT	
	5D		PAYOUT	
			PAYOUT	
			PAYOUT	
PLACES PAID OUT			NUMBER OF ENTRIES	

Rodeo Racing / Jackpot

NAME	

SANCTION / ASSOCIATION		DATE		TIME	:
LOCATION		MILES AWAY			
ENTRY FEE	$	ADDED MONEY	$		
SIDE POT Y/N TYPE		ENTRY FEE	$	ADDED MONEY	$
SIDE POT Y/N TYPE		ENTRY FEE	$	ADDED MONEY	$
TIME OUTS ALLOWED	○ YES ○ NO	STALLS AVAILABLE	○ YES ○ NO	FEE	$
ENTER: ON SITE / CALL IN DATE		TIME	:	PHONE	
BUDDY		CONFIRMATION #		CALL BACK	
DRAW					

HEALTH REQUIREMENTS

GATE		RUN IN / SET UP	
GROUND TYPE			
GROUND CONDITION			
POSITION ON THE GROUND			
WEATHER CONDITIONS			
TEMPERATURE		SLACK / PERFORMANCE	
INDOOR / OUTDOOR		DAYLIGHT / LIGHTED	
OTHER PEN NOTES			

RESULTS

WINNING TIME	1D		PAYOUT	
	2D		PAYOUT	
	3D		PAYOUT	
	4D		PAYOUT	
	5D		PAYOUT	
			PAYOUT	
			PAYOUT	
PLACES PAID OUT			NUMBER OF ENTRIES	

Rodeo Racing / Jackpot

NAME			
SANCTION / ASSOCIATION		DATE	TIME :
LOCATION		MILES AWAY	
ENTRY FEE	$	ADDED MONEY	$
SIDE POT Y/N TYPE		ENTRY FEE $	ADDED MONEY $
SIDE POT Y/N TYPE		ENTRY FEE $	ADDED MONEY $
TIME OUTS ALLOWED	○ YES ○ NO	STALLS AVAILABLE ○ YES ○ NO	FEE $
ENTER: ON SITE / CALL IN DATE		TIME :	PHONE
BUDDY		CONFIRMATION #	CALL BACK
DRAW			

HEALTH REQUIREMENTS

GATE		RUN IN / SET UP	
GROUND TYPE			
GROUND CONDITION			
POSITION ON THE GROUND			
WEATHER CONDITIONS			
TEMPERATURE		SLACK / PERFORMANCE	
INDOOR / OUTDOOR		DAYLIGHT / LIGHTED	
OTHER PEN NOTES			

RESULTS

WINNING TIME	1D		PAYOUT	
	2D		PAYOUT	
	3D		PAYOUT	
	4D		PAYOUT	
	5D		PAYOUT	
			PAYOUT	
			PAYOUT	
PLACES PAID OUT			NUMBER OF ENTRIES	

Rodeo Racing / Jackpot

NAME	

SANCTION / ASSOCIATION		DATE		TIME	:
LOCATION		MILES AWAY			
ENTRY FEE	$	ADDED MONEY	$		
SIDE POT Y/N TYPE		ENTRY FEE	$	ADDED MONEY	$
SIDE POT Y/N TYPE		ENTRY FEE	$	ADDED MONEY	$
TIME OUTS ALLOWED	○ YES ○ NO	STALLS AVAILABLE	○ YES ○ NO	FEE	$
ENTER: ON SITE / CALL IN DATE		TIME	:	PHONE	
BUDDY		CONFIRMATION #		CALL BACK	
DRAW					

HEALTH REQUIREMENTS

GATE		RUN IN / SET UP	
GROUND TYPE			
GROUND CONDITION			
POSITION ON THE GROUND			
WEATHER CONDITIONS			
TEMPERATURE		SLACK / PERFORMANCE	
INDOOR / OUTDOOR		DAYLIGHT / LIGHTED	
OTHER PEN NOTES			

RESULTS				
WINNING TIME	ID		PAYOUT	
	2D		PAYOUT	
	3D		PAYOUT	
	4D		PAYOUT	
	5D		PAYOUT	
			PAYOUT	
			PAYOUT	
PLACES PAID OUT			NUMBER OF ENTRIES	

Rodeo Racing / Jackpot

NAME					
SANCTION / ASSOCIATION		DATE		TIME	:
LOCATION		MILES AWAY			
ENTRY FEE	$	ADDED MONEY	$		
SIDE POT Y/N TYPE		ENTRY FEE	$	ADDED MONEY	$
SIDE POT Y/N TYPE		ENTRY FEE	$	ADDED MONEY	$
TIME OUTS ALLOWED	○ YES ○ NO	STALLS AVAILABLE	○ YES ○ NO	FEE	$
ENTER: ON SITE / CALL IN DATE		TIME	:	PHONE	
BUDDY		CONFIRMATION #		CALL BACK	
DRAW					

HEALTH REQUIREMENTS

GATE		RUN IN / SET UP	
GROUND TYPE			
GROUND CONDITION			
POSITION ON THE GROUND			
WEATHER CONDITIONS			
TEMPERATURE		SLACK / PERFORMANCE	
INDOOR / OUTDOOR		DAYLIGHT / LIGHTED	
OTHER PEN NOTES			

RESULTS

WINNING TIME	ID		PAYOUT	
	1D		PAYOUT	
	2D		PAYOUT	
	3D		PAYOUT	
	4D		PAYOUT	
	5D		PAYOUT	
			PAYOUT	
			PAYOUT	
PLACES PAID OUT			NUMBER OF ENTRIES	

Rodeo Racing / Jackpot

NAME	

SANCTION / ASSOCIATION		DATE		TIME	:
LOCATION		MILES AWAY			
ENTRY FEE	$	ADDED MONEY	$		
SIDE POT Y/N TYPE		ENTRY FEE	$	ADDED MONEY	$
SIDE POT Y/N TYPE		ENTRY FEE	$	ADDED MONEY	$
TIME OUTS ALLOWED	○ YES ○ NO	STALLS AVAILABLE	○ YES ○ NO	FEE	$
ENTER: ON SITE / CALL IN DATE		TIME	:	PHONE	
BUDDY		CONFIRMATION #		CALL BACK	
DRAW					

HEALTH REQUIREMENTS

GATE		RUN IN / SET UP	
GROUND TYPE			
GROUND CONDITION			
POSITION ON THE GROUND			
WEATHER CONDITIONS			
TEMPERATURE		SLACK / PERFORMANCE	
INDOOR / OUTDOOR		DAYLIGHT / LIGHTED	
OTHER PEN NOTES			

RESULTS

WINNING TIME	1D		PAYOUT	
	2D		PAYOUT	
	3D		PAYOUT	
	4D		PAYOUT	
	5D		PAYOUT	
			PAYOUT	
			PAYOUT	
PLACES PAID OUT			NUMBER OF ENTRIES	

Rodeo Racing / Jackpot

NAME	

SANCTION / ASSOCIATION		DATE		TIME	:
LOCATION		MILES AWAY			
ENTRY FEE	$	ADDED MONEY	$		
SIDE POT Y/N TYPE		ENTRY FEE	$	ADDED MONEY	$
SIDE POT Y/N TYPE		ENTRY FEE	$	ADDED MONEY	$
TIME OUTS ALLOWED	○ YES ○ NO	STALLS AVAILABLE	○ YES ○ NO	FEE	$
ENTER: ON SITE / CALL IN DATE		TIME	:	PHONE	
BUDDY		CONFIRMATION #		CALL BACK	
DRAW					

HEALTH REQUIREMENTS

GATE		RUN IN / SET UP	
GROUND TYPE			
GROUND CONDITION			
POSITION ON THE GROUND			
WEATHER CONDITIONS			
TEMPERATURE		SLACK / PERFORMANCE	
INDOOR / OUTDOOR		DAYLIGHT / LIGHTED	
OTHER PEN NOTES			

RESULTS

WINNING TIME	1)		PAYOUT	
	2)		PAYOUT	
	3)		PAYOUT	
	4)		PAYOUT	
	5)		PAYOUT	
			PAYOUT	
			PAYOUT	
PLACES PAID OUT			NUMBER OF ENTRIES	

Rodeo Racing / Jackpot

NAME	

SANCTION / ASSOCIATION		DATE		TIME	:
LOCATION		MILES AWAY			
ENTRY FEE	$	ADDED MONEY	$		
SIDE POT Y/N TYPE		ENTRY FEE	$	ADDED MONEY	$
SIDE POT Y/N TYPE		ENTRY FEE	$	ADDED MONEY	$
TIME OUTS ALLOWED	○ YES ○ NO	STALLS AVAILABLE	○ YES ○ NO	FEE	$
ENTER: ON SITE / CALL IN DATE		TIME	:	PHONE	
BUDDY		CONFIRMATION #		CALL BACK	
DRAW					

HEALTH REQUIREMENTS

GATE		RUN IN / SET UP	
GROUND TYPE			
GROUND CONDITION			
POSITION ON THE GROUND			
WEATHER CONDITIONS			
TEMPERATURE		SLACK / PERFORMANCE	
INDOOR / OUTDOOR		DAYLIGHT / LIGHTED	
OTHER PEN NOTES			

RESULTS

WINNING TIME	ID			
	2D		PAYOUT	
	3D		PAYOUT	
	4D		PAYOUT	
	5D		PAYOUT	
			PAYOUT	
			PAYOUT	
			PAYOUT	
PLACES PAID OUT			NUMBER OF ENTRIES	

Rodeo Racing / Jackpot

NAME	

SANCTION / ASSOCIATION		DATE		TIME	:
LOCATION		MILES AWAY			
ENTRY FEE	$	ADDED MONEY	$		
SIDE POT Y/N TYPE		ENTRY FEE	$	ADDED MONEY	$
SIDE POT Y/N TYPE		ENTRY FEE	$	ADDED MONEY	$
TIME OUTS ALLOWED	○ YES ○ NO	STALLS AVAILABLE	○ YES ○ NO	FEE	$
ENTER: ON SITE / CALL IN DATE		TIME	:	PHONE	
BUDDY		CONFIRMATION #		CALL BACK	
DRAW					

HEALTH REQUIREMENTS

GATE		RUN IN / SET UP	
GROUND TYPE			
GROUND CONDITION			
POSITION ON THE GROUND			
WEATHER CONDITIONS			
TEMPERATURE		SLACK / PERFORMANCE	
INDOOR / OUTDOOR		DAYLIGHT / LIGHTED	
OTHER PEN NOTES			

RESULTS

WINNING TIME	ID		PAYOUT	
	2D		PAYOUT	
	3D		PAYOUT	
	4D		PAYOUT	
	5D		PAYOUT	
			PAYOUT	
			PAYOUT	
PLACES PAID OUT			NUMBER OF ENTRIES	

Rodeo Racing / Jackpot

NAME	

SANCTION / ASSOCIATION		DATE		TIME	:
LOCATION		MILES AWAY			
ENTRY FEE	$	ADDED MONEY	$		
SIDE POT Y/N TYPE		ENTRY FEE	$	ADDED MONEY	$
SIDE POT Y/N TYPE		ENTRY FEE	$	ADDED MONEY	$
TIME OUTS ALLOWED	○ YES ○ NO	STALLS AVAILABLE	○ YES ○ NO	FEE	$
ENTER: ON SITE / CALL IN DATE		TIME	:	PHONE	
BUDDY		CONFIRMATION #		CALL BACK	
DRAW					

HEALTH REQUIREMENTS	

GATE		RUN IN / SET UP	
GROUND TYPE			
GROUND CONDITION			
POSITION ON THE GROUND			
WEATHER CONDITIONS			
TEMPERATURE		SLACK / PERFORMANCE	
INDOOR / OUTDOOR		DAYLIGHT / LIGHTED	
OTHER PEN NOTES			

RESULTS

WINNING TIME	ID		PAYOUT	
	2D		PAYOUT	
	3D		PAYOUT	
	4D		PAYOUT	
	5D		PAYOUT	
			PAYOUT	
			PAYOUT	
PLACES PAID OUT			NUMBER OF ENTRIES	

Rodeo Racing / Jackpot

NAME	

SANCTION / ASSOCIATION		DATE		TIME	:
LOCATION		MILES AWAY			
ENTRY FEE	$	ADDED MONEY	$		
SIDE POT Y/N TYPE		ENTRY FEE	$	ADDED MONEY	$
SIDE POT Y/N TYPE		ENTRY FEE	$	ADDED MONEY	$
TIME OUTS ALLOWED	○ YES ○ NO	STALLS AVAILABLE	○ YES ○ NO	FEE	$
ENTER: ON SITE / CALL IN DATE		TIME	:	PHONE	
BUDDY		CONFIRMATION #		CALL BACK	
DRAW					

HEALTH REQUIREMENTS

GATE		RUN IN / SET UP	
GROUND TYPE			
GROUND CONDITION			
POSITION ON THE GROUND			
WEATHER CONDITIONS			
TEMPERATURE		SLACK / PERFORMANCE	
INDOOR / OUTDOOR		DAYLIGHT / LIGHTED	
OTHER PEN NOTES			

RESULTS

WINNING TIME	ID		PAYOUT	
	2D		PAYOUT	
	3D		PAYOUT	
	4D		PAYOUT	
	5D		PAYOUT	
			PAYOUT	
			PAYOUT	
PLACES PAID OUT			NUMBER OF ENTRIES	

Rodeo Racing / Jackpot

NAME	

SANCTION / ASSOCIATION		DATE		TIME	:
LOCATION		MILES AWAY			
ENTRY FEE	$	ADDED MONEY	$		
SIDE POT Y/N TYPE		ENTRY FEE	$	ADDED MONEY	$
SIDE POT Y/N TYPE		ENTRY FEE	$	ADDED MONEY	$
TIME OUTS ALLOWED	○ YES ○ NO	STALLS AVAILABLE	○ YES ○ NO	FEE	$
ENTER: ON SITE / CALL IN DATE		TIME	:	PHONE	
BUDDY		CONFIRMATION #		CALL BACK	
DRAW					

HEALTH REQUIREMENTS

GATE		RUN IN / SET UP	
GROUND TYPE			
GROUND CONDITION			
POSITION ON THE GROUND			
WEATHER CONDITIONS			
TEMPERATURE		SLACK / PERFORMANCE	
INDOOR / OUTDOOR		DAYLIGHT / LIGHTED	
OTHER PEN NOTES			

RESULTS

WINNING TIME	ID		PAYOUT	
	2D		PAYOUT	
	3D		PAYOUT	
	4D		PAYOUT	
	5D		PAYOUT	
			PAYOUT	
			PAYOUT	
PLACES PAID OUT			NUMBER OF ENTRIES	

Rodeo Racing / Jackpot

NAME	

SANCTION / ASSOCIATION		DATE		TIME	:
LOCATION		MILES AWAY			
ENTRY FEE	$	ADDED MONEY	$		
SIDE POT Y/N TYPE		ENTRY FEE	$	ADDED MONEY	$
SIDE POT Y/N TYPE		ENTRY FEE	$	ADDED MONEY	$
TIME OUTS ALLOWED	○ YES ○ NO	STALLS AVAILABLE	○ YES ○ NO	FEE	$
ENTER: ON SITE / CALL IN DATE		TIME	:	PHONE	
BUDDY		CONFIRMATION #		CALL BACK	
DRAW					

HEALTH REQUIREMENTS

GATE		RUN IN / SET UP	
GROUND TYPE			
GROUND CONDITION			
POSITION ON THE GROUND			
WEATHER CONDITIONS			
TEMPERATURE		SLACK / PERFORMANCE	
INDOOR / OUTDOOR		DAYLIGHT / LIGHTED	
OTHER PEN NOTES			

RESULTS					
WINNING TIME	1D		PAYOUT		
	2D		PAYOUT		
	3D		PAYOUT		
	4D		PAYOUT		
	5D		PAYOUT		
			PAYOUT		
			PAYOUT		
PLACES PAID OUT			NUMBER OF ENTRIES		

Rodeo Racing / Jackpot

NAME	

SANCTION / ASSOCIATION		DATE		TIME	:
LOCATION		MILES AWAY			
ENTRY FEE	$	ADDED MONEY	$		
SIDE POT Y/N TYPE		ENTRY FEE	$	ADDED MONEY	$
SIDE POT Y/N TYPE		ENTRY FEE	$	ADDED MONEY	$
TIME OUTS ALLOWED	○ YES ○ NO	STALLS AVAILABLE	○ YES ○ NO	FEE	$
ENTER: ON SITE / CALL IN DATE		TIME	:	PHONE	
BUDDY		CONFIRMATION #		CALL BACK	
DRAW					

HEALTH REQUIREMENTS

GATE		RUN IN / SET UP	
GROUND TYPE			
GROUND CONDITION			
POSITION ON THE GROUND			
WEATHER CONDITIONS			
TEMPERATURE		SLACK / PERFORMANCE	
INDOOR / OUTDOOR		DAYLIGHT / LIGHTED	
OTHER PEN NOTES			

RESULTS

WINNING TIME	ID		PAYOUT	
	2D		PAYOUT	
	3D		PAYOUT	
	4D		PAYOUT	
	5D		PAYOUT	
			PAYOUT	
			PAYOUT	
PLACES PAID OUT			NUMBER OF ENTRIES	

Rodeo Racing / Jackpot

NAME	

SANCTION / ASSOCIATION		DATE		TIME	:
LOCATION		MILES AWAY			
ENTRY FEE	$	ADDED MONEY	$		
SIDE POT Y/N TYPE		ENTRY FEE	$	ADDED MONEY	$
SIDE POT Y/N TYPE		ENTRY FEE	$	ADDED MONEY	$
TIME OUTS ALLOWED	○ YES ○ NO	STALLS AVAILABLE	○ YES ○ NO	FEE	$
ENTER: ON SITE / CALL IN DATE		TIME	:	PHONE	
BUDDY		CONFIRMATION #		CALL BACK	
DRAW					

HEALTH REQUIREMENTS

GATE		RUN IN / SET UP	
GROUND TYPE			
GROUND CONDITION			
POSITION ON THE GROUND			
WEATHER CONDITIONS			
TEMPERATURE		SLACK / PERFORMANCE	
INDOOR / OUTDOOR		DAYLIGHT / LIGHTED	
OTHER PEN NOTES			

RESULTS

WINNING TIME				
	1D		PAYOUT	
	2D		PAYOUT	
	3D		PAYOUT	
	4D		PAYOUT	
	5D		PAYOUT	
			PAYOUT	
			PAYOUT	
PLACES PAID OUT		NUMBER OF ENTRIES		

Rodeo Racing / Jackpot

NAME	

SANCTION / ASSOCIATION		DATE		TIME	:
LOCATION		MILES AWAY			
ENTRY FEE	$	ADDED MONEY	$		
SIDE POT Y/N TYPE		ENTRY FEE	$	ADDED MONEY	$
SIDE POT Y/N TYPE		ENTRY FEE	$	ADDED MONEY	$
TIME OUTS ALLOWED	○ YES ○ NO	STALLS AVAILABLE	○ YES ○ NO	FEE	$
ENTER: ON SITE / CALL IN DATE		TIME	:	PHONE	
BUDDY		CONFIRMATION #		CALL BACK	
DRAW					

HEALTH REQUIREMENTS

GATE		RUN IN / SET UP	
GROUND TYPE			
GROUND CONDITION			
POSITION ON THE GROUND			
WEATHER CONDITIONS			
TEMPERATURE		SLACK / PERFORMANCE	
INDOOR / OUTDOOR		DAYLIGHT / LIGHTED	
OTHER PEN NOTES			

RESULTS					
WINNING TIME	1D		PAYOUT		
	2D		PAYOUT		
	3D		PAYOUT		
	4D		PAYOUT		
	5D		PAYOUT		
			PAYOUT		
			PAYOUT		
PLACES PAID OUT			NUMBER OF ENTRIES		

Rodeo Racing / Jackpot

NAME	

SANCTION / ASSOCIATION		DATE		TIME	:
LOCATION		MILES AWAY			
ENTRY FEE	$	ADDED MONEY	$		
SIDE POT Y/N TYPE		ENTRY FEE	$	ADDED MONEY	$
SIDE POT Y/N TYPE		ENTRY FEE	$	ADDED MONEY	$
TIME OUTS ALLOWED	○ YES ○ NO	STALLS AVAILABLE	○ YES ○ NO	FEE	$
ENTER: ON SITE / CALL IN DATE		TIME	:	PHONE	
BUDDY		CONFIRMATION #		CALL BACK	
DRAW					

HEALTH REQUIREMENTS

GATE	
GROUND TYPE	
GROUND CONDITION	
POSITION ON THE GROUND	
WEATHER CONDITIONS	
TEMPERATURE	
INDOOR / OUTDOOR	
OTHER PEN NOTES	

RUN IN / SET UP	
SLACK / PERFORMANCE	
DAYLIGHT / LIGHTED	

RESULTS

WINNING TIME	ID			
	1D		PAYOUT	
	2D		PAYOUT	
	3D		PAYOUT	
	4D		PAYOUT	
	5D		PAYOUT	
			PAYOUT	
			PAYOUT	
PLACES PAID OUT			NUMBER OF ENTRIES	

Rodeo Racing / Jackpot

NAME	

SANCTION / ASSOCIATION		DATE		TIME	:
LOCATION		MILES AWAY			
ENTRY FEE	$	ADDED MONEY	$		
SIDE POT Y/N TYPE		ENTRY FEE	$	ADDED MONEY	$
SIDE POT Y/N TYPE		ENTRY FEE	$	ADDED MONEY	$
TIME OUTS ALLOWED	○ YES ○ NO	STALLS AVAILABLE	○ YES ○ NO	FEE	$
ENTER: ON SITE / CALL IN DATE		TIME	:	PHONE	
BUDDY		CONFIRMATION #		CALL BACK	
DRAW					

HEALTH REQUIREMENTS

GATE		RUN IN / SET UP	
GROUND TYPE			
GROUND CONDITION			
POSITION ON THE GROUND			
WEATHER CONDITIONS			
TEMPERATURE		SLACK / PERFORMANCE	
INDOOR / OUTDOOR		DAYLIGHT / LIGHTED	
OTHER PEN NOTES			

RESULTS

WINNING TIME	ID		PAYOUT	
	2D		PAYOUT	
	3D		PAYOUT	
	4D		PAYOUT	
	5D		PAYOUT	
			PAYOUT	
			PAYOUT	
PLACES PAID OUT			NUMBER OF ENTRIES	

Rodeo Racing / Jackpot

NAME	

SANCTION / ASSOCIATION		DATE		TIME	:
LOCATION		MILES AWAY			
ENTRY FEE	$	ADDED MONEY	$		
SIDE POT Y/N TYPE		ENTRY FEE	$	ADDED MONEY	$
SIDE POT Y/N TYPE		ENTRY FEE	$	ADDED MONEY	$
TIME OUTS ALLOWED	○ YES ○ NO	STALLS AVAILABLE	○ YES ○ NO	FEE	$
ENTER: ON SITE / CALL IN DATE		TIME	:	PHONE	
BUDDY		CONFIRMATION #		CALL BACK	
DRAW					

HEALTH REQUIREMENTS

GATE	
GROUND TYPE	
GROUND CONDITION	
POSITION ON THE GROUND	
WEATHER CONDITIONS	
TEMPERATURE	
INDOOR / OUTDOOR	
OTHER PEN NOTES	

RUN IN / SET UP	
SLACK / PERFORMANCE	
DAYLIGHT / LIGHTED	

RESULTS

WINNING TIME	ID		PAYOUT	
	1)		PAYOUT	
	2)		PAYOUT	
	3)		PAYOUT	
	4)		PAYOUT	
	5)		PAYOUT	
			PAYOUT	
			PAYOUT	

PLACES PAID OUT		NUMBER OF ENTRIES	

Rodeo Racing / Jackpot

NAME	

SANCTION / ASSOCIATION		DATE		TIME	:
LOCATION		MILES AWAY			
ENTRY FEE	$	ADDED MONEY	$		
SIDE POT Y/N TYPE		ENTRY FEE	$	ADDED MONEY	$
SIDE POT Y/N TYPE		ENTRY FEE	$	ADDED MONEY	$
TIME OUTS ALLOWED	○ YES ○ NO	STALLS AVAILABLE	○ YES ○ NO	FEE	$
ENTER: ON SITE / CALL IN DATE		TIME	:	PHONE	
BUDDY		CONFIRMATION #		CALL BACK	
DRAW					

HEALTH REQUIREMENTS

GATE		RUN IN / SET UP	
GROUND TYPE			
GROUND CONDITION			
POSITION ON THE GROUND			
WEATHER CONDITIONS			
TEMPERATURE		SLACK / PERFORMANCE	
INDOOR / OUTDOOR		DAYLIGHT / LIGHTED	
OTHER PEN NOTES			

RESULTS

WINNING TIME	ID		PAYOUT	
	2D		PAYOUT	
	3D		PAYOUT	
	4D		PAYOUT	
	5D		PAYOUT	
			PAYOUT	
			PAYOUT	
PLACES PAID OUT			NUMBER OF ENTRIES	

Rodeo Racing / Jackpot

NAME					
SANCTION / ASSOCIATION		DATE		TIME	:
LOCATION		MILES AWAY			
ENTRY FEE	$	ADDED MONEY	$		
SIDE POT Y/N TYPE		ENTRY FEE	$	ADDED MONEY	$
SIDE POT Y/N TYPE		ENTRY FEE	$	ADDED MONEY	$
TIME OUTS ALLOWED	○ YES ○ NO	STALLS AVAILABLE	○ YES ○ NO	FEE	$
ENTER: ON SITE / CALL IN DATE		TIME	:	PHONE	
BUDDY		CONFIRMATION #		CALL BACK	
DRAW					

HEALTH REQUIREMENTS

GATE		RUN IN / SET UP	
GROUND TYPE			
GROUND CONDITION			
POSITION ON THE GROUND			
WEATHER CONDITIONS			
TEMPERATURE		SLACK / PERFORMANCE	
INDOOR / OUTDOOR		DAYLIGHT / LIGHTED	
OTHER PEN NOTES			

RESULTS

WINNING TIME			PAYOUT	
	1D		PAYOUT	
	2D		PAYOUT	
	3D		PAYOUT	
	4D		PAYOUT	
	5D		PAYOUT	
			PAYOUT	
			PAYOUT	
PLACES PAID OUT			NUMBER OF ENTRIES	

Rodeo Racing / Jackpot

NAME	

SANCTION / ASSOCIATION		DATE		TIME	:
LOCATION		MILES AWAY			
ENTRY FEE	$	ADDED MONEY	$		
SIDE POT Y/N TYPE		ENTRY FEE	$	ADDED MONEY	$
SIDE POT Y/N TYPE		ENTRY FEE	$	ADDED MONEY	$
TIME OUTS ALLOWED	○ YES ○ NO	STALLS AVAILABLE	○ YES ○ NO	FEE	$
ENTER: ON SITE / CALL IN DATE		TIME	:	PHONE	
BUDDY		CONFIRMATION #		CALL BACK	
DRAW					

HEALTH REQUIREMENTS

GATE		RUN IN / SET UP	
GROUND TYPE			
GROUND CONDITION			
POSITION ON THE GROUND			
WEATHER CONDITIONS			
TEMPERATURE		SLACK / PERFORMANCE	
INDOOR / OUTDOOR		DAYLIGHT / LIGHTED	
OTHER PEN NOTES			

RESULTS

WINNING TIME			PAYOUT	
	1D		PAYOUT	
	2D		PAYOUT	
	3D		PAYOUT	
	4D		PAYOUT	
	5D		PAYOUT	
			PAYOUT	
			PAYOUT	
PLACES PAID OUT			NUMBER OF ENTRIES	

Rodeo Racing / Jackpot

NAME	

SANCTION / ASSOCIATION		DATE		TIME	:
LOCATION		MILES AWAY			
ENTRY FEE	$	ADDED MONEY	$		
SIDE POT Y/N TYPE		ENTRY FEE	$	ADDED MONEY	$
SIDE POT Y/N TYPE		ENTRY FEE	$	ADDED MONEY	$
TIME OUTS ALLOWED	○ YES ○ NO	STALLS AVAILABLE	○ YES ○ NO	FEE	$
ENTER: ON SITE / CALL IN DATE		TIME	:	PHONE	
BUDDY		CONFIRMATION #		CALL BACK	
DRAW					

HEALTH REQUIREMENTS

GATE		RUN IN / SET UP	
GROUND TYPE			
GROUND CONDITION			
POSITION ON THE GROUND			
WEATHER CONDITIONS			
TEMPERATURE		SLACK / PERFORMANCE	
INDOOR / OUTDOOR		DAYLIGHT / LIGHTED	
OTHER PEN NOTES			

RESULTS

WINNING TIME	ID		PAYOUT	
	2D		PAYOUT	
	3D		PAYOUT	
	4D		PAYOUT	
	5D		PAYOUT	
			PAYOUT	
			PAYOUT	

PLACES PAID OUT		NUMBER OF ENTRIES	

Rodeo Racing / Jackpot

NAME	

SANCTION / ASSOCIATION		DATE		TIME	:
LOCATION		MILES AWAY			
ENTRY FEE	$	ADDED MONEY	$		
SIDE POT Y/N TYPE		ENTRY FEE	$	ADDED MONEY	$
SIDE POT Y/N TYPE		ENTRY FEE	$	ADDED MONEY	$
TIME OUTS ALLOWED	○ YES ○ NO	STALLS AVAILABLE	○ YES ○ NO	FEE	$
ENTER: ON SITE / CALL IN DATE		TIME	:	PHONE	
BUDDY		CONFIRMATION #		CALL BACK	
DRAW					

HEALTH REQUIREMENTS

GATE		RUN IN / SET UP	
GROUND TYPE			
GROUND CONDITION			
POSITION ON THE GROUND			
WEATHER CONDITIONS			
TEMPERATURE		SLACK / PERFORMANCE	
INDOOR / OUTDOOR		DAYLIGHT / LIGHTED	
OTHER PEN NOTES			

RESULTS

WINNING TIME	ID		PAYOUT	
	2D		PAYOUT	
	3D		PAYOUT	
	4D		PAYOUT	
	5D		PAYOUT	
			PAYOUT	
			PAYOUT	
PLACES PAID OUT			NUMBER OF ENTRIES	

Rodeo Racing / Jackpot

NAME					
SANCTION / ASSOCIATION		DATE		TIME	:
LOCATION		MILES AWAY			
ENTRY FEE	$	ADDED MONEY	$		
SIDE POT Y/N TYPE		ENTRY FEE	$	ADDED MONEY	$
SIDE POT Y/N TYPE		ENTRY FEE	$	ADDED MONEY	$
TIME OUTS ALLOWED	○ YES ○ NO	STALLS AVAILABLE	○ YES ○ NO	FEE	$
ENTER: ON SITE / CALL IN DATE		TIME	:	PHONE	
BUDDY		CONFIRMATION #		CALL BACK	
DRAW					

HEALTH REQUIREMENTS

GATE		RUN IN / SET UP	
GROUND TYPE			
GROUND CONDITION			
POSITION ON THE GROUND			
WEATHER CONDITIONS			
TEMPERATURE		SLACK / PERFORMANCE	
INDOOR / OUTDOOR		DAYLIGHT / LIGHTED	
OTHER PEN NOTES			

RESULTS				
WINNING TIME	1D		PAYOUT	
	2D		PAYOUT	
	3D		PAYOUT	
	4D		PAYOUT	
	5D		PAYOUT	
			PAYOUT	
			PAYOUT	
PLACES PAID OUT			NUMBER OF ENTRIES	

Rodeo Racing / Jackpot

NAME	

SANCTION / ASSOCIATION		DATE		TIME	:
LOCATION		MILES AWAY			
ENTRY FEE	$	ADDED MONEY	$		
SIDE POT Y/N TYPE		ENTRY FEE	$	ADDED MONEY	$
SIDE POT Y/N TYPE		ENTRY FEE	$	ADDED MONEY	$
TIME OUTS ALLOWED	○ YES ○ NO	STALLS AVAILABLE	○ YES ○ NO	FEE	$
ENTER: ON SITE / CALL IN DATE		TIME	:	PHONE	
BUDDY		CONFIRMATION #		CALL BACK	
DRAW					

HEALTH REQUIREMENTS

GATE		RUN IN / SET UP	
GROUND TYPE			
GROUND CONDITION			
POSITION ON THE GROUND			
WEATHER CONDITIONS			
TEMPERATURE		SLACK / PERFORMANCE	
INDOOR / OUTDOOR		DAYLIGHT / LIGHTED	
OTHER PEN NOTES			

RESULTS

WINNING TIME	ID		PAYOUT	
	2D		PAYOUT	
	3D		PAYOUT	
	4D		PAYOUT	
	5D		PAYOUT	
			PAYOUT	
			PAYOUT	

PLACES PAID OUT		NUMBER OF ENTRIES	

Rodeo Racing / Jackpot

NAME	

SANCTION / ASSOCIATION		DATE		TIME	:
LOCATION		MILES AWAY			
ENTRY FEE	$	ADDED MONEY	$		
SIDE POT Y/N TYPE		ENTRY FEE	$	ADDED MONEY	$
SIDE POT Y/N TYPE		ENTRY FEE	$	ADDED MONEY	$
TIME OUTS ALLOWED	○ YES ○ NO	STALLS AVAILABLE	○ YES ○ NO	FEE	$
ENTER: ON SITE / CALL IN DATE		TIME	:	PHONE	
BUDDY		CONFIRMATION #		CALL BACK	
DRAW					

HEALTH REQUIREMENTS

GATE		RUN IN / SET UP	
GROUND TYPE			
GROUND CONDITION			
POSITION ON THE GROUND			
WEATHER CONDITIONS			
TEMPERATURE		SLACK / PERFORMANCE	
INDOOR / OUTDOOR		DAYLIGHT / LIGHTED	
OTHER PEN NOTES			

RESULTS

WINNING TIME				
	1)		PAYOUT	
	2)		PAYOUT	
	3)		PAYOUT	
	4)		PAYOUT	
	5)		PAYOUT	
			PAYOUT	
			PAYOUT	
PLACES PAID OUT			NUMBER OF ENTRIES	

Rodeo Racing / Jackpot

NAME	

SANCTION / ASSOCIATION		DATE		TIME	:
LOCATION		MILES AWAY			
ENTRY FEE	$	ADDED MONEY	$		
SIDE POT Y/N TYPE		ENTRY FEE	$	ADDED MONEY	$
SIDE POT Y/N TYPE		ENTRY FEE	$	ADDED MONEY	$
TIME OUTS ALLOWED	○ YES ○ NO	STALLS AVAILABLE	○ YES ○ NO	FEE	$
ENTER: ON SITE / CALL IN DATE		TIME	:	PHONE	
BUDDY		CONFIRMATION #		CALL BACK	
DRAW					

HEALTH REQUIREMENTS

GATE		RUN IN / SET UP	
GROUND TYPE			
GROUND CONDITION			
POSITION ON THE GROUND			
WEATHER CONDITIONS			
TEMPERATURE		SLACK / PERFORMANCE	
INDOOR / OUTDOOR		DAYLIGHT / LIGHTED	
OTHER PEN NOTES			

RESULTS

WINNING TIME	ID		PAYOUT	
	2D		PAYOUT	
	3D		PAYOUT	
	4D		PAYOUT	
	5D		PAYOUT	
			PAYOUT	
			PAYOUT	
PLACES PAID OUT			NUMBER OF ENTRIES	

Rodeo Racing / Jackpot

NAME					
SANCTION / ASSOCIATION		DATE		TIME	:
LOCATION		MILES AWAY			
ENTRY FEE	$	ADDED MONEY	$		
SIDE POT Y/N TYPE		ENTRY FEE	$	ADDED MONEY	$
SIDE POT Y/N TYPE		ENTRY FEE	$	ADDED MONEY	$
TIME OUTS ALLOWED	○ YES ○ NO	STALLS AVAILABLE	○ YES ○ NO	FEE	$
ENTER: ON SITE / CALL IN DATE		TIME	:	PHONE	
BUDDY		CONFIRMATION #		CALL BACK	
DRAW					

HEALTH REQUIREMENTS

GATE		RUN IN / SET UP	
GROUND TYPE			
GROUND CONDITION			
POSITION ON THE GROUND			
WEATHER CONDITIONS			
TEMPERATURE		SLACK / PERFORMANCE	
INDOOR / OUTDOOR		DAYLIGHT / LIGHTED	
OTHER PEN NOTES			

RESULTS

WINNING TIME	ID		PAYOUT	
	1D		PAYOUT	
	2D		PAYOUT	
	3D		PAYOUT	
	4D		PAYOUT	
	5D		PAYOUT	
			PAYOUT	
			PAYOUT	
PLACES PAID OUT			NUMBER OF ENTRIES	

Rodeo Racing / Jackpot

NAME	

SANCTION / ASSOCIATION		DATE		TIME	:
LOCATION		MILES AWAY			
ENTRY FEE	$	ADDED MONEY	$		
SIDE POT Y/N TYPE		ENTRY FEE	$	ADDED MONEY	$
SIDE POT Y/N TYPE		ENTRY FEE	$	ADDED MONEY	$
TIME OUTS ALLOWED	○ YES ○ NO	STALLS AVAILABLE	○ YES ○ NO	FEE	$
ENTER: ON SITE / CALL IN DATE		TIME	:	PHONE	
BUDDY		CONFIRMATION #		CALL BACK	
DRAW					

HEALTH REQUIREMENTS

GATE		RUN IN / SET UP	
GROUND TYPE			
GROUND CONDITION			
POSITION ON THE GROUND			
WEATHER CONDITIONS			
TEMPERATURE		SLACK / PERFORMANCE	
INDOOR / OUTDOOR		DAYLIGHT / LIGHTED	
OTHER PEN NOTES			

RESULTS

WINNING TIME	ID		PAYOUT	
	2D		PAYOUT	
	3D		PAYOUT	
	4D		PAYOUT	
	5D		PAYOUT	
			PAYOUT	
			PAYOUT	
PLACES PAID OUT			NUMBER OF ENTRIES	

Rodeo Racing / Jackpot

NAME	

SANCTION / ASSOCIATION		DATE		TIME	:
LOCATION		MILES AWAY			
ENTRY FEE	$	ADDED MONEY	$		
SIDE POT Y/N TYPE		ENTRY FEE	$	ADDED MONEY	$
SIDE POT Y/N TYPE		ENTRY FEE	$	ADDED MONEY	$
TIME OUTS ALLOWED	○ YES ○ NO	STALLS AVAILABLE	○ YES ○ NO	FEE	$
ENTER: ON SITE / CALL IN DATE		TIME	:	PHONE	
BUDDY		CONFIRMATION #		CALL BACK	
DRAW					

HEALTH REQUIREMENTS

GATE	
GROUND TYPE	
GROUND CONDITION	
POSITION ON THE GROUND	
WEATHER CONDITIONS	
TEMPERATURE	
INDOOR / OUTDOOR	
OTHER PEN NOTES	

RUN IN / SET UP	
SLACK / PERFORMANCE	
DAYLIGHT / LIGHTED	

RESULTS

WINNING TIME				
	1D		PAYOUT	
	2D		PAYOUT	
	3D		PAYOUT	
	4D		PAYOUT	
	5D		PAYOUT	
			PAYOUT	
			PAYOUT	
PLACES PAID OUT			NUMBER OF ENTRIES	

Rodeo Racing / Jackpot

NAME	

SANCTION / ASSOCIATION		DATE		TIME	:
LOCATION		MILES AWAY			
ENTRY FEE	$	ADDED MONEY	$		
SIDE POT Y/N TYPE		ENTRY FEE	$	ADDED MONEY	$
SIDE POT Y/N TYPE		ENTRY FEE	$	ADDED MONEY	$
TIME OUTS ALLOWED	○ YES ○ NO	STALLS AVAILABLE	○ YES ○ NO	FEE	$
ENTER: ON SITE / CALL IN DATE		TIME	:	PHONE	
BUDDY		CONFIRMATION #		CALL BACK	
DRAW					

HEALTH REQUIREMENTS

GATE		RUN IN / SET UP	
GROUND TYPE			
GROUND CONDITION			
POSITION ON THE GROUND			
WEATHER CONDITIONS			
TEMPERATURE		SLACK / PERFORMANCE	
INDOOR / OUTDOOR		DAYLIGHT / LIGHTED	
OTHER PEN NOTES			

RESULTS

WINNING TIME	ID		PAYOUT	
	2D		PAYOUT	
	3D		PAYOUT	
	4D		PAYOUT	
	5D		PAYOUT	
			PAYOUT	
			PAYOUT	
PLACES PAID OUT			NUMBER OF ENTRIES	

Rodeo Racing / Jackpot

NAME	

SANCTION / ASSOCIATION		DATE		TIME	:
LOCATION		MILES AWAY			
ENTRY FEE	$	ADDED MONEY	$		
SIDE POT Y/N TYPE		ENTRY FEE	$	ADDED MONEY	$
SIDE POT Y/N TYPE		ENTRY FEE	$	ADDED MONEY	$
TIME OUTS ALLOWED	○ YES ○ NO	STALLS AVAILABLE	○ YES ○ NO	FEE	$
ENTER: ON SITE / CALL IN DATE		TIME	:	PHONE	
BUDDY		CONFIRMATION #		CALL BACK	
DRAW					

HEALTH REQUIREMENTS

GATE		RUN IN / SET UP	
GROUND TYPE			
GROUND CONDITION			
POSITION ON THE GROUND			
WEATHER CONDITIONS			
TEMPERATURE		SLACK / PERFORMANCE	
INDOOR / OUTDOOR		DAYLIGHT / LIGHTED	
OTHER PEN NOTES			

RESULTS				
WINNING TIME	1D		PAYOUT	
	2D		PAYOUT	
	3D		PAYOUT	
	4D		PAYOUT	
	5D		PAYOUT	
			PAYOUT	
			PAYOUT	
PLACES PAID OUT			NUMBER OF ENTRIES	

Rodeo Racing / Jackpot

NAME	

SANCTION / ASSOCIATION		DATE		TIME	:
LOCATION		MILES AWAY			
ENTRY FEE	$	ADDED MONEY	$		
SIDE POT Y/N TYPE		ENTRY FEE	$	ADDED MONEY	$
SIDE POT Y/N TYPE		ENTRY FEE	$	ADDED MONEY	$
TIME OUTS ALLOWED	○ YES ○ NO	STALLS AVAILABLE	○ YES ○ NO	FEE	$
ENTER: ON SITE / CALL IN DATE		TIME	:	PHONE	
BUDDY		CONFIRMATION #		CALL BACK	
DRAW					

HEALTH REQUIREMENTS

GATE		RUN IN / SET UP	
GROUND TYPE			
GROUND CONDITION			
POSITION ON THE GROUND			
WEATHER CONDITIONS			
TEMPERATURE		SLACK / PERFORMANCE	
INDOOR / OUTDOOR		DAYLIGHT / LIGHTED	
OTHER PEN NOTES			

RESULTS

WINNING TIME			PAYOUT	
	1D		PAYOUT	
	2D		PAYOUT	
	3D		PAYOUT	
	4D		PAYOUT	
	5D		PAYOUT	
			PAYOUT	
			PAYOUT	
PLACES PAID OUT			NUMBER OF ENTRIES	

Rodeo Racing / Jackpot

NAME						
SANCTION / ASSOCIATION		DATE		TIME		:
LOCATION		MILES AWAY				
ENTRY FEE	$	ADDED MONEY	$			
SIDE POT Y/N TYPE		ENTRY FEE	$	ADDED MONEY	$	
SIDE POT Y/N TYPE		ENTRY FEE	$	ADDED MONEY	$	
TIME OUTS ALLOWED	○ YES ○ NO	STALLS AVAILABLE	○ YES ○ NO	FEE	$	
ENTER: ON SITE / CALL IN DATE		TIME	:	PHONE		
BUDDY		CONFIRMATION #		CALL BACK		
DRAW						

HEALTH REQUIREMENTS	

GATE		RUN IN / SET UP	
GROUND TYPE			
GROUND CONDITION			
POSITION ON THE GROUND			
WEATHER CONDITIONS			
TEMPERATURE		SLACK / PERFORMANCE	
INDOOR / OUTDOOR		DAYLIGHT / LIGHTED	
OTHER PEN NOTES			

RESULTS

WINNING TIME	1D		PAYOUT	
	2D		PAYOUT	
	3D		PAYOUT	
	4D		PAYOUT	
	5D		PAYOUT	
			PAYOUT	
			PAYOUT	
PLACES PAID OUT			NUMBER OF ENTRIES	

Rodeo Racing / Jackpot

NAME	

SANCTION / ASSOCIATION		DATE		TIME	:
LOCATION		MILES AWAY			
ENTRY FEE	$	ADDED MONEY	$		
SIDE POT Y/N TYPE		ENTRY FEE	$	ADDED MONEY	$
SIDE POT Y/N TYPE		ENTRY FEE	$	ADDED MONEY	$
TIME OUTS ALLOWED	○ YES ○ NO	STALLS AVAILABLE	○ YES ○ NO	FEE	$
ENTER: ON SITE / CALL IN DATE		TIME	:	PHONE	
BUDDY		CONFIRMATION #		CALL BACK	
DRAW					

HEALTH REQUIREMENTS

GATE		RUN IN / SET UP	
GROUND TYPE			
GROUND CONDITION			
POSITION ON THE GROUND			
WEATHER CONDITIONS			
TEMPERATURE		SLACK / PERFORMANCE	
INDOOR / OUTDOOR		DAYLIGHT / LIGHTED	
OTHER PEN NOTES			

RESULTS

WINNING TIME	ID		PAYOUT	
	2D		PAYOUT	
	3D		PAYOUT	
	4D		PAYOUT	
	5D		PAYOUT	
			PAYOUT	
			PAYOUT	
PLACES PAID OUT			NUMBER OF ENTRIES	

Rodeo Racing / Jackpot

NAME	

SANCTION / ASSOCIATION		DATE		TIME	:
LOCATION		MILES AWAY			
ENTRY FEE	$	ADDED MONEY	$		
SIDE POT Y/N TYPE		ENTRY FEE	$	ADDED MONEY	$
SIDE POT Y/N TYPE		ENTRY FEE	$	ADDED MONEY	$
TIME OUTS ALLOWED	○ YES ○ NO	STALLS AVAILABLE	○ YES ○ NO	FEE	$
ENTER: ON SITE / CALL IN DATE		TIME	:	PHONE	
BUDDY		CONFIRMATION #		CALL BACK	
DRAW					

HEALTH REQUIREMENTS	

GATE		RUN IN / SET UP	
GROUND TYPE			
GROUND CONDITION			
POSITION ON THE GROUND			
WEATHER CONDITIONS			
TEMPERATURE		SLACK / PERFORMANCE	
INDOOR / OUTDOOR		DAYLIGHT / LIGHTED	
OTHER PEN NOTES			

RESULTS				
WINNING TIME	ID		PAYOUT	
	2D		PAYOUT	
	3D		PAYOUT	
	4D		PAYOUT	
	5D		PAYOUT	
			PAYOUT	
			PAYOUT	
PLACES PAID OUT			NUMBER OF ENTRIES	

Rodeo Racing / Jackpot

NAME	

SANCTION / ASSOCIATION		DATE		TIME	:
LOCATION		MILES AWAY			
ENTRY FEE	$	ADDED MONEY	$		
SIDE POT Y/N TYPE		ENTRY FEE	$	ADDED MONEY	$
SIDE POT Y/N TYPE		ENTRY FEE	$	ADDED MONEY	$
TIME OUTS ALLOWED	○ YES ○ NO	STALLS AVAILABLE	○ YES ○ NO	FEE	$
ENTER: ON SITE / CALL IN DATE		TIME	:	PHONE	
BUDDY		CONFIRMATION #		CALL BACK	
DRAW					

HEALTH REQUIREMENTS

GATE		RUN IN / SET UP	
GROUND TYPE			
GROUND CONDITION			
POSITION ON THE GROUND			
WEATHER CONDITIONS			
TEMPERATURE		SLACK / PERFORMANCE	
INDOOR / OUTDOOR		DAYLIGHT / LIGHTED	
OTHER PEN NOTES			

RESULTS

WINNING TIME				
	1D		PAYOUT	
	2D		PAYOUT	
	3D		PAYOUT	
	4D		PAYOUT	
	5D		PAYOUT	
			PAYOUT	
			PAYOUT	
PLACES PAID OUT			NUMBER OF ENTRIES	

Rodeo Racing / Jackpot

NAME	

SANCTION / ASSOCIATION		DATE		TIME	:
LOCATION		MILES AWAY			
ENTRY FEE	$	ADDED MONEY	$		
SIDE POT Y/N TYPE		ENTRY FEE	$	ADDED MONEY	$
SIDE POT Y/N TYPE		ENTRY FEE	$	ADDED MONEY	$
TIME OUTS ALLOWED	○ YES ○ NO	STALLS AVAILABLE	○ YES ○ NO	FEE	$
ENTER: ON SITE / CALL IN DATE		TIME	:	PHONE	
BUDDY		CONFIRMATION #		CALL BACK	
DRAW					

HEALTH REQUIREMENTS

GATE		RUN IN / SET UP	
GROUND TYPE			
GROUND CONDITION			
POSITION ON THE GROUND			
WEATHER CONDITIONS			
TEMPERATURE		SLACK / PERFORMANCE	
INDOOR / OUTDOOR		DAYLIGHT / LIGHTED	
OTHER PEN NOTES			

RESULTS

WINNING TIME	ID		PAYOUT	
	2D		PAYOUT	
	3D		PAYOUT	
	4D		PAYOUT	
	5D		PAYOUT	
			PAYOUT	
			PAYOUT	
PLACES PAID OUT			NUMBER OF ENTRIES	

Rodeo Racing / Jackpot

NAME	

SANCTION / ASSOCIATION		DATE		TIME	:
LOCATION		MILES AWAY			
ENTRY FEE	$	ADDED MONEY	$		
SIDE POT Y/N TYPE		ENTRY FEE	$	ADDED MONEY	$
SIDE POT Y/N TYPE		ENTRY FEE	$	ADDED MONEY	$
TIME OUTS ALLOWED	○ YES ○ NO	STALLS AVAILABLE	○ YES ○ NO	FEE	$
ENTER: ON SITE / CALL IN DATE		TIME	:	PHONE	
BUDDY		CONFIRMATION #		CALL BACK	
DRAW					

HEALTH REQUIREMENTS

GATE		RUN IN / SET UP	
GROUND TYPE			
GROUND CONDITION			
POSITION ON THE GROUND			
WEATHER CONDITIONS			
TEMPERATURE		SLACK / PERFORMANCE	
INDOOR / OUTDOOR		DAYLIGHT / LIGHTED	
OTHER PEN NOTES			

RESULTS

WINNING TIME	ID		PAYOUT	
	2D		PAYOUT	
	3D		PAYOUT	
	4D		PAYOUT	
	5D		PAYOUT	
			PAYOUT	
			PAYOUT	
PLACES PAID OUT			NUMBER OF ENTRIES	

Rodeo Racing / Jackpot

NAME					
SANCTION / ASSOCIATION		DATE		TIME	:
LOCATION		MILES AWAY			
ENTRY FEE	$	ADDED MONEY	$		
SIDE POT Y/N TYPE		ENTRY FEE	$	ADDED MONEY	$
SIDE POT Y/N TYPE		ENTRY FEE	$	ADDED MONEY	$
TIME OUTS ALLOWED	○ YES ○ NO	STALLS AVAILABLE	○ YES ○ NO	FEE	$
ENTER: ON SITE / CALL IN DATE		TIME	:	PHONE	
BUDDY		CONFIRMATION #		CALL BACK	
DRAW					

HEALTH REQUIREMENTS

GATE	
GROUND TYPE	
GROUND CONDITION	
POSITION ON THE GROUND	
WEATHER CONDITIONS	
TEMPERATURE	
INDOOR / OUTDOOR	
OTHER PEN NOTES	

RUN IN / SET UP	
SLACK / PERFORMANCE	
DAYLIGHT / LIGHTED	

RESULTS

WINNING TIME				
	1D		PAYOUT	
	2D		PAYOUT	
	3D		PAYOUT	
	4D		PAYOUT	
	5D		PAYOUT	
			PAYOUT	
			PAYOUT	
PLACES PAID OUT			NUMBER OF ENTRIES	

Rodeo Racing / Jackpot

NAME	

SANCTION / ASSOCIATION		DATE		TIME	:
LOCATION		MILES AWAY			
ENTRY FEE	$	ADDED MONEY	$		
SIDE POT Y/N TYPE		ENTRY FEE	$	ADDED MONEY	$
SIDE POT Y/N TYPE		ENTRY FEE	$	ADDED MONEY	$
TIME OUTS ALLOWED	○ YES ○ NO	STALLS AVAILABLE	○ YES ○ NO	FEE	$
ENTER: ON SITE / CALL IN DATE		TIME	:	PHONE	
BUDDY		CONFIRMATION #		CALL BACK	
DRAW					

HEALTH REQUIREMENTS

GATE	
GROUND TYPE	
GROUND CONDITION	
POSITION ON THE GROUND	
WEATHER CONDITIONS	
TEMPERATURE	
INDOOR / OUTDOOR	
OTHER PEN NOTES	

RUN IN / SET UP	
SLACK / PERFORMANCE	
DAYLIGHT / LIGHTED	

RESULTS

WINNING TIME	ID		PAYOUT	
	2D		PAYOUT	
	3D		PAYOUT	
	4D		PAYOUT	
	5D		PAYOUT	
			PAYOUT	
			PAYOUT	
PLACES PAID OUT			NUMBER OF ENTRIES	

Rodeo Racing / Jackpot

NAME					
SANCTION / ASSOCIATION		DATE		TIME	:
LOCATION		MILES AWAY			
ENTRY FEE	$	ADDED MONEY	$		
SIDE POT Y/N TYPE		ENTRY FEE	$	ADDED MONEY	$
SIDE POT Y/N TYPE		ENTRY FEE	$	ADDED MONEY	$
TIME OUTS ALLOWED	○ YES ○ NO	STALLS AVAILABLE	○ YES ○ NO	FEE	$
ENTER: ON SITE / CALL IN DATE		TIME	:	PHONE	
BUDDY		CONFIRMATION #		CALL BACK	
DRAW					

HEALTH REQUIREMENTS	

GATE		RUN IN / SET UP	
GROUND TYPE			
GROUND CONDITION			
POSITION ON THE GROUND			
WEATHER CONDITIONS			
TEMPERATURE		SLACK / PERFORMANCE	
INDOOR / OUTDOOR		DAYLIGHT / LIGHTED	
OTHER PEN NOTES			

RESULTS

WINNING TIME	1D		PAYOUT	
	2D		PAYOUT	
	3D		PAYOUT	
	4D		PAYOUT	
	5D		PAYOUT	
			PAYOUT	
			PAYOUT	
PLACES PAID OUT			NUMBER OF ENTRIES	

Rodeo Racing / Jackpot

NAME	

SANCTION / ASSOCIATION		DATE		TIME	:
LOCATION		MILES AWAY			
ENTRY FEE	$	ADDED MONEY	$		
SIDE POT Y/N TYPE		ENTRY FEE	$	ADDED MONEY	$
SIDE POT Y/N TYPE		ENTRY FEE	$	ADDED MONEY	$
TIME OUTS ALLOWED	○ YES ○ NO	STALLS AVAILABLE	○ YES ○ NO	FEE	$
ENTER: ON SITE / CALL IN DATE		TIME	:	PHONE	
BUDDY		CONFIRMATION #		CALL BACK	
DRAW					

HEALTH REQUIREMENTS

GATE		RUN IN / SET UP	
GROUND TYPE			
GROUND CONDITION			
POSITION ON THE GROUND			
WEATHER CONDITIONS			
TEMPERATURE		SLACK / PERFORMANCE	
INDOOR / OUTDOOR		DAYLIGHT / LIGHTED	
OTHER PEN NOTES			

RESULTS

WINNING TIME	ID		PAYOUT	
	2D		PAYOUT	
	3D		PAYOUT	
	4D		PAYOUT	
	5D		PAYOUT	
			PAYOUT	
			PAYOUT	
PLACES PAID OUT			NUMBER OF ENTRIES	

Rodeo Racing / Jackpot

NAME	

SANCTION / ASSOCIATION		DATE		TIME	:
LOCATION		MILES AWAY			
ENTRY FEE	$	ADDED MONEY	$		
SIDE POT Y/N TYPE		ENTRY FEE	$	ADDED MONEY	$
SIDE POT Y/N TYPE		ENTRY FEE	$	ADDED MONEY	$
TIME OUTS ALLOWED	○ YES ○ NO	STALLS AVAILABLE	○ YES ○ NO	FEE	$
ENTER: ON SITE / CALL IN DATE		TIME	:	PHONE	
BUDDY		CONFIRMATION #		CALL BACK	
DRAW					

HEALTH REQUIREMENTS

DATE		RUN IN / SET UP	
GROUND TYPE			
GROUND CONDITION			
POSITION ON THE GROUND			
WEATHER CONDITIONS			
TEMPERATURE		SLACK / PERFORMANCE	
INDOOR / OUTDOOR		DAYLIGHT / LIGHTED	
OTHER PEN NOTES			

RESULTS

WINNING TIME	ID		PAYOUT	
	2D		PAYOUT	
	3D		PAYOUT	
	4D		PAYOUT	
	5D		PAYOUT	
			PAYOUT	
			PAYOUT	

PLACES PAID OUT		NUMBER OF ENTRIES	

Rodeo Racing / Jackpot

NAME	

SANCTION / ASSOCIATION		DATE		TIME	:
LOCATION		MILES AWAY			
ENTRY FEE	$	ADDED MONEY	$		
SIDE POT Y/N TYPE		ENTRY FEE	$	ADDED MONEY	$
SIDE POT Y/N TYPE		ENTRY FEE	$	ADDED MONEY	$
TIME OUTS ALLOWED	○ YES ○ NO	STALLS AVAILABLE	○ YES ○ NO	FEE	$
ENTER: ON SITE / CALL IN DATE		TIME	:	PHONE	
BUDDY		CONFIRMATION #		CALL BACK	
DRAW					

HEALTH REQUIREMENTS

GATE		RUN IN / SET UP	
GROUND TYPE			
GROUND CONDITION			
POSITION ON THE GROUND			
WEATHER CONDITIONS			
TEMPERATURE		SLACK / PERFORMANCE	
INDOOR / OUTDOOR		DAYLIGHT / LIGHTED	
OTHER PEN NOTES			

RESULTS

WINNING TIME	ID		PAYOUT	
	2D		PAYOUT	
	3D		PAYOUT	
	4D		PAYOUT	
	5D		PAYOUT	
			PAYOUT	
			PAYOUT	
PLACES PAID OUT			NUMBER OF ENTRIES	

Rodeo Racing / Jackpot

NAME	

SANCTION / ASSOCIATION		DATE		TIME	:
LOCATION		MILES AWAY			
ENTRY FEE	$	ADDED MONEY	$		
SIDE POT Y/N TYPE		ENTRY FEE	$	ADDED MONEY	$
SIDE POT Y/N TYPE		ENTRY FEE	$	ADDED MONEY	$
TIME OUTS ALLOWED	○ YES ○ NO	STALLS AVAILABLE	○ YES ○ NO	FEE	$
ENTER: ON SITE / CALL IN DATE		TIME	:	PHONE	
BUDDY		CONFIRMATION #		CALL BACK	
DRAW					

HEALTH REQUIREMENTS

GATE	
GROUND TYPE	
GROUND CONDITION	
POSITION ON THE GROUND	
WEATHER CONDITIONS	
TEMPERATURE	
INDOOR / OUTDOOR	
OTHER PEN NOTES	

RUN IN / SET UP	
SLACK / PERFORMANCE	
DAYLIGHT / LIGHTED	

RESULTS

WINNING TIME				
	1D		PAYOUT	
	2D		PAYOUT	
	3D		PAYOUT	
	4D		PAYOUT	
	5D		PAYOUT	
			PAYOUT	
			PAYOUT	
PLACES PAID OUT			NUMBER OF ENTRIES	

Rodeo Racing / Jackpot

NAME	

SANCTION / ASSOCIATION		DATE		TIME	:
LOCATION		MILES AWAY			
ENTRY FEE	$	ADDED MONEY	$		
SIDE POT Y/N TYPE		ENTRY FEE	$	ADDED MONEY	$
SIDE POT Y/N TYPE		ENTRY FEE	$	ADDED MONEY	$
TIME OUTS ALLOWED	○ YES ○ NO	STALLS AVAILABLE	○ YES ○ NO	FEE	$
ENTER: ON SITE / CALL IN DATE		TIME	:	PHONE	
BUDDY		CONFIRMATION #		CALL BACK	
DRAW					

HEALTH REQUIREMENTS

GATE		RUN IN / SET UP	
GROUND TYPE			
GROUND CONDITION			
POSITION ON THE GROUND			
WEATHER CONDITIONS			
TEMPERATURE		SLACK / PERFORMANCE	
INDOOR / OUTDOOR		DAYLIGHT / LIGHTED	
OTHER PEN NOTES			

RESULTS				
WINNING TIME	ID		PAYOUT	
	2D		PAYOUT	
	3D		PAYOUT	
	4D		PAYOUT	
	5D		PAYOUT	
			PAYOUT	
			PAYOUT	
PLACES PAID OUT			NUMBER OF ENTRIES	

www.ingramcontent.com/pod-product-compliance
Lightning Source LLC
Chambersburg PA
CBHW081233080526
44587CB00022B/3930